A Travelling Quaker Writes ...

(Volume One)

by

Dewi Heald

First published by Dream Jellyhouse in print on demand in 2019. 2nd typeset in June 2019

ISBN 978-1-9160241-0-6

Dream Jellyhouse

Dedication

"The most interesting Ministry is not the Ministry that you agree with, it is the Ministry that you disagree with."

(Ministry in Cardiff Quaker Meeting, c.2016)

I hope that all readers find plenty to disagree with among these pages.

However, this book can only be dedicated to the people who I have met on my Quaker travels, every one of them a true Friend.

Table of Contents

1. What is this book all about?

Thank you for picking up this book and looking at the first chapter. Of course, I would hope that you have bought a copy and made a donation to the Cardiff Quaker Meeting House Appeal (there is a page about that at the end of the book) but however and wherever you are looking at it, I think that I ought to tell you a little bit about it before you commit to reading on past the first paragraph.

Still here? Good. I hope that this book will be read by Quakers and non-Quakers alike. If you are not a Quaker and you are worried about the terminology involved, then the second chapter 'What is a Quaker?' tries to put everything in context for you. I also hope that my thoughts and writings will appeal to those who are interested in spiritual matters in general and that no-one feels that they have to be a Quaker to understand what I am writing about.

Why then is this 'A Travelling Quaker Writes'? The purpose of my travels is to visit every Quaker Meeting House[1] in the UK. There are over four hundred of them[2], so I have set myself the time limit of forty years for completing this task.

Some people respond to this by asking me about my travels, some people respond by asking me why and

---

[1] There are going to be a lot of footnotes, by the way. They will say things like – a Meeting House is just that, a place where Quakers meet. Long ago these would have been in ordinary houses and hence the name. Nowadays they tend to be buildings specifically for that purpose, though Quakers can worship anywhere.

[2] At the time of publication, I have visited twenty Meeting Houses – 380 to go! Only twelve are written about in this book, my apologies to the people whose Meetings I have missed out – Bath, Fareham, Reading, Lancaster, Lampeter, Liverpool, Bridgend and South Belfast.

some people respond to this by asking me what a Quaker is. If you are still asking the third question, then I repeat that the next chapter is for you. Actually, read that chapter even if you know what a Quaker is.

As a summary, I am a Quaker and Quakers meet in buildings known as Meeting Houses. There are four hundred of them in the UK and I am visiting all of them. This is the first edition of the book, covering twelve, but I hope that one day it will include all four hundred (by which time it will be a big book and you will be thoroughly bored of reading the same introduction to each one).

I hope that if you are not a Quaker, you will still gain some pleasure and insight from this. Each visit is followed by some thoughts and ideas in chapters called 'One Quaker and ...' There is a set of (very good) books called 'Twelve Quakers and ...' and if you want to know what twelve Quakers think of these subjects then read those. This is just one person's view and that person is me.

I do need to explain the comment I made at the start about the Meeting House Appeal – this book is written to raise money for the Cardiff Meeting House appeal. How to give money to this appeal is in the back of this book. However, please bear in mind that very little of the cost of a book is profit for the author. In other words, if you paid £4.99 for this book then you have probably just given 75p to the Appeal. Sorry, all the rest goes to Amazon and the websites that do the actual printing. In other words, if you enjoy this book, please do not be offended by the further begging at the end.

RANDOMLY ASKED QUESTIONS (RAQ)

Do your travels have a plan?

No, most definitely not. In fact, I think that a plan would make it about ticking off Meetings from a list and I would prefer to think of it as travelling to where I am needed, when I am needed. This is one reason why it will take forty years to complete. If you are not familiar with Quakers, then a 'Meeting' is like a church and its congregation combined. If you are familiar with Quakers, then do not complain about that description.

There is a tradition among Quakers of visiting each other's Meetings, giving greetings from your own Meeting and then returning with greetings from the Meeting visited. My 'home meeting' (if there is such a thing) is Cardiff, by the way. I imagine that in the days when Quakers were few and far between and regularly persecuted, a visit from another Meeting could ensure solidarity as much as anything.

In the next chapter, I will tell you that I am only able to offer simple answers that are largely unsatisfactory. How about this as an answer then - 'I do not have a plan, God has a plan'?

By the way, because I hope that you do not have to be religious or even spiritual to find something of interest in this book, so you may have to forgive me when I write things like that.

Why write about it?

Every now and then I would return to Meeting in Cardiff and tell them about the Meeting that I had visited. Rather than just say 'I bring greetings from ...', I liked to give some detail or learning point from the visit as a way of sharing knowledge about different Meetings. People would then say to me 'why don't you write all this down?' I did intend to do so, given that I write about enough other things.

However, the real impetus to start on this project came from the Cardiff Meeting House Appeal. Cardiff Meeting occupies an old Victorian building (some say a former vicarage) in Cardiff city centre. In terms of location it is fantastic. In terms of everything else it is looking rather faded. There is a Meeting Room on the ground floor and then the upper floors are rented out to voluntary sector projects and used as meeting rooms (small 'm' there, of course[3]). In many ways, it is a lovely building that receives much use but in other ways it is a problem for the Meeting.

By 2016, there was quite a backlog of repairs and updates needed – some rooms simply needed heating, let alone any kind of refurbishment. The Meeting decided to raise money for an overall refurbishment and the changing of a number of elements such as the entrance hall and kitchen facilities which would make it more hospitable. The original proposal was to build a new Meeting room on the back of the building. I found this proposal to be inspiring and ambitious and was very much in favour of it. However, I did acknowledge that the price tag for even the most basic refurb - £200,000 – required a lot of fundraising and so the Appeal aims towards the first stage

[3] Some people like me use 'Meeting' to mean a Quaker Meeting but 'meeting' to mean any other meeting. Capitalisation is everything in religion!

of a plan that may yet have a more ambitious sequel (like this book).

Having learned how to self-publish in the meantime, the two ideas seemed natural bedfellows. I would write a book about my Quaker travels and it would raise money for the Meeting House appeal.

Will you ever complete the project?

Sometimes the point of the journey is to travel rather than to arrive. There are a number of UK train companies who may have misunderstood that concept.

Is the book in chronological order?

No, most definitely not. It is written in an order that will hopefully make for good reading rather than being in order. It is not even about all the Meetings that I have visited.

Will this book give me a history of Quaker worship in various places?

Most definitely not. There are plenty of books about Quaker history, written by people far more knowledgeable than me. As an example, the chapter in this book based around Yealand Conyers will tell you almost nothing about Yealand Conyers itself, but it will tell you my thoughts about being met by people at strange railway stations. This is more of a travel memoir than a history.

What is a Quaker?

You are looking for the next chapter.

2. What is a Quaker?[4]

It was my third date with Samantha (not her real name). We had talked about music, we had talked about politics, we had even talked about whether the 'Fifty Shades of Grey' books were accurate but there was one thing that we had not talked about. I waited for the question that can make or break any relationship –

"What is a Quaker?"

It is no good replying that Quakers are a very diverse group of people because the next question is "What do Quakers believe?" and you have to explain that being a Quaker is not like signing up to a belief system in the way that you do in other religions. Questions about Quakers tend not to have easy answers. My mother (her real name) once questioned the nature of Quaker Meetings by asking, "Who teaches you?" and I could only think to reply, "God teaches us." This was not a good enough answer.

However, I would like this book to be accessible to non-Quakers and Quakers alike. I am not sure that anyone has ever changed their beliefs as a result of knowing me, but I hope that they have at least had a few answers to some of their questions or perhaps a few new questions to answer. This means that before we start travelling, I need to explain a little about who Quakers are and what they believe. This will also include some terminology to help with what follows.

Some readers may choose to skip the rest of this chapter.

However, for everyone else –

"What is a Quaker?"

You can probably find a hundred or more different definitions but here is mine. The Religious Society of Friends (Quakers)[5] is a movement that started in the mid seventeenth century with a man named George Fox.

That terminology is worth pausing on for a moment as you are going to hear reference to the Religious Society of Friends again and because Quakers often refer to each other as 'Friends'. I believe that it was originally intended as 'friend of the truth' but there is still a wonderful feeling to be had when you walk into a roomful of strangers and they greet you as 'friend'. The chapter on Streatham & Brixton Meeting deals with this in more detail.

George Fox and the early Quakers believed that mainstream Christian religion (which was really the only type available) had gone astray and that religion needed to be taken back to its roots. I have often heard Quakers referred to as having much in common with first century Christians, before the development of churches, chapels and power structures and when followers of Christ were taken to be equals in their quest.

To this day, Quakers worship by gathering in a 'Meeting House' and sitting in silence until one or other is inspired to speak. Anyone can speak, as the Spirit may choose to speak through any one of us (and this is referred to as 'ministry'). There is no priesthood or rather, everyone is a priest and has the potential to speak. Sometimes Quaker

---

[5] The Religious Society of Friends is the official name.

Meetings[6] pass in silence, sometimes they are full of thoughtful comment or 'Ministry'. There is no direct argument and people do not repeat what they have said once they have spoken. Time is always taken for people to think and reflect on what they have heard. Although there have been some changes such as the length of time Quakers meet for, the basic structure of 'Meeting for Worship' remains the same.

The ideas of Quakerism spread across Britain and Ireland and to the emerging states in the USA. Quakers were seen as a threat to both church and state and were persecuted. In Britain they were often imprisoned and in the colonies of America they were sometimes executed for being Quakers. It is worth noting that the American Quakers have different forms of worship, but we will come to that later in the book or possibly in another book (American publishers wanting to pay for me to write about American Meetings please note). For now, we will stay with the British 'silent worship' tradition.

In time, Quakers made a name for themselves in business, partly as traditional careers in politics, religion and the armed forces were not open to them. Quakers were banned from attending university as well. However, they did have a reputation for honesty and this is what lies behind Quaker success in the manufacture of chocolate - at a time when there were no laws to regulate the production of chocolate, you could trust the Cadburys, Rowntrees and Frys to be honest about what they were selling you. This was true in other businesses too.

I am conscious of leaving out a lot of history but the twentieth century saw two developments which will help to answer the 'What is a Quaker?' question. The first is

---

[6] 'Meeting' has two uses – it is the physical space like a church but also the people who meet like a congregation.

that Quaker testimonies were brought together into the format - Peace, Equality, Simplicity and Truth. Some people like to add Environment to that as well ... you will gain the impression that Quakers have a lot of differing opinions and that this is welcomed rather than condemned.

In a sense, all the testimonies are just attempts to express more simply the beliefs that Quakers have always had. Quakers believe that everyone has 'that of God' in them and therefore, we are all equal and there is no hierarchy. You can tell immediately that this puts Quakers in the forefront of issues such as marriage equality and gender equality. Equality does really mean equality and there are some fascinating stories from the early centuries of Quaker marriages which scandalised society by upholding the principle that wife and husband are equals.

Taking this equality principle further, if there is that of God in everyone, then how can you take another life? This refusal to destroy God's creation (extended in many cases to the environment, though you will find many Quaker carnivores as well as vegetarians or vegans) leads to the peace testimony and long-standing campaigns against the arms trade, war and weapons (though we will talk about the wider implications of pacifism in a later chapter).

If you are going to reject the ostentation of vast cathedrals, then simplicity also makes sense. We worship God with what we do in our lives, not with the buildings that we build in his name. There is a Quaker saying that what you say on a Sunday should not be different to what you do on a Monday. In other words, if you have a belief then you should live it.

Simplicity is often taken to mean not being caught up in the external trappings and glories of the material world. It did once mean plain dress and when I first attended a Quaker Meeting I was worried that my colourful clothes might be frowned upon. Not only were they not, but I soon learnt that Quakers were not the type to frown on people full stop.

I mentioned the reputation for honesty, this is partly because the Quaker way is also a plainness of speech where you should try to say what you mean without relying on complicated or misleading formulations that deceive people.

That leads us to the final testimony, truth. Once again, we will look at this in more detail later on but, for now, it will do to say that Quakers believe in not just telling the truth but acting honestly. One of my favourite examples is the Quaker protestor who stood outside an arms fayre asking all those attending, "Are you aware that what you are doing is against the works of Jesus Christ?" That probably sounds quite harmless, but Quakers have been arrested for protesting and are still being arrested to this day. Not all of them feel called to protest, but the Society values both those who pray and those who protest.

Before introducing the four testimonies, I said that there were two things that gave a sharper focus to Quakerism in the twentieth century and I think that the other one needs to be mentioned – the First World War.

You can imagine that in Victorian times, a respectable businessman or businesswoman could feel quite content being a Quaker. There were Quaker Meeting Houses[7] established in many places and the persecution had largely ended. Quakers were still involved in unpopular causes such as gender equality and tackling poverty, but there was no need for the previous secrecy or insecurity.

You could say that Quakers were tolerated and even comfortable with their existence.

One historian puts the impact of the First World War for Quakers as being to take away all that comfort and security and force them to stand in opposition to the very state which they had become accustomed to upholding. There were other movements within the Society and any Quakers who are still reading will doubtless be finding this summary too simple, but I would not under-rate the stand that Quakers took in the First World War. One interesting point to note is that they were offered an exemption from conscription but refused to support it on the grounds that it should be offered to everyone and not just to Quakers. Equality in action, indeed.

Reading the history, I realised that there was a fascinating patchwork of responses among Quakers at the time. We tend to forget now that there were plenty of Quakers who joined up to fight, declaring that duty to country was more important than the pacifism testimony. I have read that as many as 25% of all Quakers attending Meetings in 1914 went to fight in the War. You will not find that statistic commonly repeated, but some Quakers did fight (and factories such as Cadburys kept jobs open for those who went to fight).

Then there were the Quakers who joined the Friends Ambulance Unit and showed great courage in providing medical support on the front line without actually fighting. Finally, there were the conscientious objectors who refused to be involved at all. They were certainly not regarded as heroic in this stance at the time and there are some fine cartoons from the period held at the Quaker Study Centre in Birmingham showing the derision shown by some towards those who would not fight.

You can read more about this in the chapter on pacifism but, for now, I think that you cannot understand modern Quakers and their commitments (and radical spirit on occasions) without seeing how much the First World War disrupted some of the previous thinking.

This mixed response to the First World War also sums up something essential to me about being a Quaker and also helps to explain why 'What is a Quaker?' is such a hard question to answer. There will be times when you can say 'Quakers believe' this or that but generally you can find a very wide range of opinions on anything. Part of the fascinating element of Quaker Worship is that all those differing views can be brought together.

I was sitting in my workplace one day and a friend (small 'f', you can see how you need to make a distinction here) said to me, "So, you're a Quaker then?" I nodded and said, "Yes, I am". There was a pause and then she added, "I don't really know what that means". Sometimes it would be tempting to reply, "Neither do I".

All I will end by saying is that if you are Quaker-curious or in any way prompted by this book to find out more then I do recommend visiting www.quakers.org and finding out where your local Meeting House is. As I found out when I was in Brixton, there is always a F/friendly welcome.

Now read on ...

3. Faringdon, Oxfordshire

"Where It All Began"

Religion is not a subject that is discussed in polite conversation in the UK. I am not saying that it is up there with crime, abortion, politics, sex or bull-fighting, but it is not something that most people talk about. I often think that the 'default position' – what people will assume if they know nothing about you – is a kind of wishy-washy atheism mixed with a vague spirituality that probably means that you complain that Christmas is too commercial and would like to get married in a church. Hardcore atheists never accept that theirs has become the default option but tell people that you are religious (not spiritual) and you will notice it soon enough. If you go to church on a Sunday people will ask you 'why?' whereas if you do not go to church on a Sunday, no-one will ask you 'why?'

I suspect that religion is worse than a taboo subject because it is about how we feel. I discussed in the introduction how to answer (or avoid answering) 'What do Quakers believe?' and that rather sums up the only way people have to talk about religion. Yet those who are religious know that it is not a list of beliefs that you sign up to in exchange for a membership card and a weekly wafer. Religion is something you feel. Discussing feelings never goes down well in polite society. It is not all that great in impolite society for that matter.

Once I had decided that I was a Quaker, I really did not tell many people. Sometimes I used the excuse of it being private, but really I was worried what they might say. Even with trusted friends I would probably avoid saying anything. You might say that my experience in Faringdon was what changed me in this regard. You might also say that it was the Spirit teaching me a valuable lesson in this regard.

Faringdon is a small town not far from Oxford. It is small enough that you can walk around it quickly and small enough that it is easy to wander into the countryside and gain an unusual view of the White Horse of Uffington in the distance. You do know that the 'white horse' is a dragon, by the way?[8]

My friend Henry, who was living in Faringdon at the time, told me that Salvador Dali once collapsed while wearing a diving suit in Faringdon High Street and I can only say that whether that it is true or not, it is one of the best claims to fame by a town that I have heard.

I had not seen Henry for a while. He had been living abroad for some years and I had never persuaded my wife that we should visit him. By the time that my wife had become my ex-wife, his circumstances had changed. I messaged him to ask, 'Can I visit you in Prague?' and received the reply, 'I'll meet you in Swindon'. Such is life.

Faringdon is a fair drive from Swindon but he picked me up at the station and we were soon chatting about the intervening years. He had had his own share of romantic troubles and you could imagine that there was a lot of thinking on how you reach the middle of your life alone and what the future might hold. We walked in the local countryside, we met some of the people who he knew locally and we enjoyed swapping stories of how life was

---

[8] It is said that a local vicar, upset that a dragon might be a pagan symbol, made sure that the village always referred to it as a horse. I recommend finding a photo of it (once you had read this chapter) and you will see what I mean – it is noticeably dragonlike.

treating us. However, we had nothing planned for the Sunday morning.

Had I been presented with a blank canvas to paint Sunday morning on, I would simply have opted for a walk in the countryside or a last visit to the local café before I headed home. However, Henry said something that surprised me. He explained that opposite his house was a small, old building belonging to an unusual group of people known as 'Quakers'. He had been there a few times and it was an interesting way to spend a Sunday morning. It was time for me to admit my secret religious identity. Ripping open my jacket to reveal a shirt with 'Q' written on it ...

It turned out that I had walked past the Quaker Meeting House in Faringdon several times without noticing it. Up to this point my experience of Meeting Houses was that they were modern or at the very least Victorian structures like the one in Cardiff. I had never seen a seventeenth century Meeting House before and I was quite taken aback by it. Thinking of Oxford with its magnificent architecture up the road, it must have been an extraordinary statement of Quaker belief in the plain and ordinary to have a little house of modest size and design with no ornamentation at all. In fact, it took me back to reading about how Meeting Houses were named after the custom of meeting in people's actual houses. This was a Meeting House that looked like nothing more than a house.

There were signs of its use over the years. Around the building was an area of green land which would have been the burial ground. As Quakers could not be buried on consecrated ground (in church cemeteries basically), many Meetings developed their own burial grounds. These can be a fascinating glimpse of the past though on this occasion any gravestones had gone (some burial grounds had no gravestones as the belief in a lack of ostentation was interpreted by some to mean no marking of burial[9]).

One of those at the Meeting pointed out the lack of windows too. There were windows, but they were comfortably over head height, a reminder, he told me, that anonymity had once been important to Quakers facing persecution and so it was important not to have windows that anyone could look into from outside.

Henry asked me at one point how books of Quaker thinking are compiled. He wondered if maybe a microphone was hung down in each Meeting House so that Ministry can be reviewed and the best of it shared with others. It sounds like a good idea, but the answer is that Ministry takes place when it takes place and for the benefit of those present. This happens in a large meeting of fifty people or in a small meeting of eight people as in Faringdon. Whatever the Spirit inspires, people will say.

Faringdon Quakers were like all the other Quakers I had met, even at an early stage in my time as a Quaker. They were genuinely friendly, welcoming and polite and you could not think of a more supportive group of people. This is probably why some people confuse 'pacifism' for 'pacific'. Quakers can be very active in their pacifism, hard as that might have been to believe in an old Meeting House in a small town in the middle of Oxfordshire where Salvador Dali once fell over in a diving suit[10].

When I returned to Cardiff Meeting, I relayed the greetings from Faringdon Meeting. One of those present

---

[9] There are different beliefs around how to mark deaths among Quakers to this day. The chapter on Quaker's Yard has more details about one of the surviving burial grounds.

[10] I am not, of course, saying that Salvador Dali fell over in the Meeting House itself, though that would be even better trivia.

said that they knew Faringdon well as it had been one of the main Meeting Houses which supported the protests at Greenham Common in the 1980s. I could remember when the American air base at Greenham Common had been surrounded by female protestors against war and nuclear proliferation but I had not realised how much support they had had from Quakers. Faringdon offered washing facilities for both women and their possessions as well as religious support and tea and biscuits. This rather unassuming building with high windows and a green bit of land had once been at the centre of radical politics.

There is an entry about the peace women of Greenham Common in Quaker Faith & Practice[11]. It is a quotation about the reasons behind the protest and why one of those who was a Quaker felt that it was necessary to be a protestor when faced with such overwhelming odds. The funny thing is that if you see Greenham Common now, it is a common again. I am not sure if we should say that the protestors won exactly, but if you think about the awesome military arsenal which was once parked there, it was inconceivable at the time that it would ever not be there. I like to think that it reminds all of us that everything is temporary, even military might.

What did I learn from this visit? It was the start of my life as a Travelling Quaker. If I was going to be a Quaker, I wanted to experience the widest variety of Meetings and I wanted to know the history and the geography of the society. More to the point, I wanted to be unafraid to say to people, 'I am going to go to a Quaker Meeting this Sunday morning'.

---

[11] QF&P – a compilation held dear by Quakers, basically a book with a collection of Quaker writing and thought from the last four hundred years

It was the beginning of an adventure, albeit one that would last a lifetime. How would people know that I was a Quaker, though? We need to talk about Quakers and visibility.

4. One Quaker and Invisibility[12]

The first time I went to a Quaker Peace and Social Witness Conference I was nervous. I had not been to any large scale Quaker gathering before and I wondered what and probably also who to expect. It was being held just outside Derby and this was quite a journey from Wales. If you are not a Quaker yourself, you may be asking what a Quaker Peace and Social Witness Conference is too. That was pretty much the position I was in. I had been asked if I wanted to be a 'QPSW correspondent' for Cardiff Meeting[13], I had agreed and then a few weeks later I was travelling to Derby.

However, I soon learnt that mealtimes were the moment to get to know other Quakers and so every breakfast, lunch and dinner I took the opportunity to join a new table and introduce myself. One lunchtime I sat next to a woman from Bangor and I was sure that when her phone had rang, she had been speaking Welsh during the call. Naturally I asked, *'Dych chi'n siarad Cymraeg?'* – 'Do you speak Welsh?' It turned out that she was a Welsh speaker and so we chatted away happily together for a few minutes in Welsh.

This was only disturbed when a man from Newbury said to me, "I thought Welsh was a dead language". Apart

[12] The views expressed in the 'One Quaker and ...' chapters are mine and mine alone and should not be taken as a statement of faith on behalf of anyone. Next time you meet a Quaker, do not challenge them with 'but it says in 'A Travelling Quaker Writes' ...'

[13] You get by now, I hope, that when I write 'Cardiff Meeting' I mean the Quaker Meeting that happens in Cardiff.

from the very obvious reply of 'clearly not', it was also a particularly annoying and rude statement from someone at a conference which claimed to celebrate inclusivity. Then again, why would he know that two people on the table spoke Welsh unless he had heard us speaking Welsh? Possibly in Newbury there are few opportunities to hear Welsh being spoken but there is also no sign that Welsh speakers hang around their necks saying 'I speak Welsh'. One of the problems for the language is that its speakers are invisible.

Are you wondering at this point if you picked up the wrong book? Firstly I am writing about a conference that I have not explained and now I am writing about minority language politics. My point is going to be that the very rude Quaker from Newbury was making a comment that could be aimed at Quakers rather than Welsh speakers.

Imagine that you are in any conversation or any social situation. You may act according to the testimonies of simplicity, truth, equality and pacifism, you may be as impressive and as thoughtful as you could ever want to be on issues of morality and conscience, but how will anyone know that you are a Quaker? On a Sunday you may even disappear to a small house in a suburban terrace or a community centre where there is not even a sign outside to show that is a place for Quakers to meet. My local Meeting House is on the same road as two churches, both of which look like places of worship and one of which will play its bells loudly on a Sunday morning (just as Meeting for Worship is about to start). You can tell that those churches are about religion, but Quakers are invisible.

Does it matter? This is a question that is never asked about the declining populations of all religions in the UK[14].

---

[14] Though I have read that attendances at cathedrals are up, but not enough to offset the declining numbers in other churches. Why cathedrals are becoming

I was struck by the suggestion in Francis Spufford's book defending Christianity, 'Unapologetic', that Christianity has been at its best when in a minority and at its worse when allied with power. However, Quakers can point to few such compromises with power or the established order. We have been a minority of outsiders since we began, but at least when we were persecuted, we were visible. How do we avoid reaching a point where no-one even notices us?

There must be scope for a compilation of reactions to someone 'coming out' as a Quaker. My own favourite is one described already, when people say 'oh, so you're a Quaker' and then pause before adding, 'I don't know what that means'. Mostly, I have found that people's knowledge of Quakers is very low and they are often surprised that Quakers even exist. There are odder reactions - my mother was once at a garden party in her home town and when she told someone that she had a son who was a Quaker, the man replied, "Quakers are all right but I don't like their attitude to homosexuality".

This hints at my first suggestion as to how to tackle the invisibility of Quakers - tell people. Religion is perhaps by its very nature a personal thing but that does not mean that it has to always be an inward thing. Does everyone know that you are a Quaker? I am not suggesting wearing a t-shirt equivalent to those wonderful LGBT campaign ones that say 'No-one knows I'm a lesbian' but I do think that those who know you best ought to know that you are a Quaker and that it is important in your life. Think about being completely honest about how your life is ordered too - when I moved house to my current location and people asked me why, I did tell them that God had guided me. Yes, people will look at you strangely when you say

---

more popular is for another book and another author.

that kind of thing, but if they are the people closest to you then they will probably still talk to you afterwards!

Oddly enough, this takes us back to Quaker Peace & Social Witness (QPSW).Despite the lack of hierarchy, there are some central organisations in Quakerism. QPSW is a UK-wide group that covers all aspects of campaigning and activism. Each Meeting will nominate a representative for it and they may choose to attend the annual conference and report back to their Meeting about some of the ongoing campaigns by other Quaker groups and Meetings. If you are trying to stop people entering an arms fair or if you are damaging fighter jets being sold to Saudi Arabia to bomb Yemen, then you are being very noticeable. Perhaps this was why I was drawn to QPSW, the feeling that it ought to matter that there are Quakers and that we ought to be seen.

This is why as well as suggesting that you tell people about being a Quaker, you also take every opportunity to celebrate the Quaker contribution to the world. Yes, Quaker Faith & Practice rightly warns us against complacency or becoming too smug about our successes (and therefore forgetting our failures), but do think about explaining to people when Quakers have made a difference. This can be locally or nationally. So, talk about the Quaker role in founding Oxfam but also what your local Meeting does to aid social causes too. We do not have a monopoly on compassion or activism, but we do still make a contribution and we should be bold in saying it.

It is too easy to forget where Quakers have made a difference. I have known Quakers say of 'Towards a Quaker View of Sex' (published in 1963) that it was only a reflection of its times. I was invited to take part in a radio discussion about religion and sexuality during 2017 and when I was asked about Quaker views, I explained that in

1963 – while homosexuality was illegal in the UK – Quakers had made the statement that the quality of a relationship was defined by whether it was abusive or not and not by the gender of those involved in it. You could hear the intake of breath in the studio. In the past, LGBT activists have told me how significant it was to have a religious organisation back the cause of equality and acceptance in 1963. We must not forget that Quakers have a history to be proud of and we need to tell others about it.

I like the badges that say 'I'm a Quaker, ask me why' and perhaps we should wear them more often. In the course of my time as a Quaker, I have investigated trying to live in a more environmentally-sustainable way. This leads to similar questions – if I buy a superb pair of non-leather shoes that look just like a pair made of leather, how will anyone know that I have made a choice to avoid leather? Does it matter?

The answer is that you buy shoelaces that say 'vegan shoes' on them. As you will read in the chapter about Swansea Meeting, I had visited the mosque on Kingsway while I worked in the city because they made an effort to connect to local organisations and people. In doing so, I had walked past the Meeting House with no idea what it was or who used it.

I cannot help but think that if Quakers are to continue to survive let alone thrive, we need to wear our Quaker laces more proudly. Perhaps it would be worth having a 'No-one Knows I'm A Quaker' t-shirt after all.

5. Birmingham Bull Street

"Quaker Renewal UK"

I have always had a fondness for Birmingham. It is a fondness born of surprise. I was brought up far away from the city and my only awareness of it was in stories of a place grim and grey with a particularly ugly shopping centre at its heart. Name the Tyne Bridge or St Paul's Cathedral or the Clifton Suspension Bridge and you know which city I am talking about. Birmingham was the second biggest city in the UK and yet no-one could name a landmark to symbolize it. I have no idea what I expected when I first visited Birmingham, but I am sure that my expectations were low.

Although stepping out on to the underground concourse of New Street station feels a little bit like entering a dark, post-apocalyptic world, Birmingham itself is a real treasure. It has a magnificent Victorian centre and cultural highlights a-plenty. When I lived in Aberystwyth I spent a long time changing trains in Birmingham and I learned to enjoy wandering out of New Street station to the attractions beyond. Go find Birmingham Cathedral and tell me where there is another Cathedral in the UK in that style.

However, I am not here to talk about cathedrals. My first visit to Birmingham for Quaker purposes was, unless you count doing the tour of the Cadbury factory at Bourneville, to attend a meeting of Quaker Renewal UK (or was that a Meeting?). I ought to explain Quaker Renewal UK as they are going to occur again in this book.

At some point in my Quaker journey (spiritual rather than geographical), I joined an online group called 'Quaker Renewal UK'. I am not sure what I expected, but I soon learned that it was the home of lively, sometimes fierce and unpacific, debate about Quaker issues. Every now and then someone would ask what 'Quaker Renewal' meant and that in itself set off a debate about what needed to be renewed and why. I learned how annoyed some people can become by candles in Quaker Meetings (really, someone left their local Meeting because of candles) and also how Quakers are no different to other human beings who use the internet to amplify their voice rather than listen. I also learned how thoughtful and fascinating others can be and found some of the truths discussed in the group truly inspiring.

During 2016-17, there was a movement to have some meetings of those taking part in Quaker Renewal UK. I thoroughly approved of this because I thought that a face to face meeting could be beneficial and also because I thought that it would be valuable to have some worship to go with the discussion.

Birmingham Bull Street was chosen as the location and I said that I would be happy to attend, though I had nowhere to stay. I did try making an obvious hint that I was looking for accommodation, but there was no response. This is not (only) sponging on my part, it is a genuine sadness that the American tradition of Quakers offering hospitality to other Quakers does not seem to exist in the UK. I would happily let any Quaker stay in my spare room (do not all come at once), so I am more than willing to re-pay or forward-pay the favour. However, on this occasion I ended up in the Premier Inn.

Bull Street was easy enough to find as the Meeting House is opposite a tram stop. Oh dear, what a missed opportunity – the tram line is only a recent innovation and Quakers should really have lobbied for that tram stop to be called 'Meeting House'.

I should probably explain that I made two visits to the Meeting House in Bull Street. On the Saturday I went to a Quaker Renewal UK Meeting and on the Sunday I went to the regular worship. The Renewal Meeting was to be a shared lunch followed by a 'long Meeting' and the regular Meeting was the same format as you will find in most UK Quaker Meetings.

At first it sounds strange to talk about a 'long Meeting'. An hour probably strikes a lot of people as a long time to spend in silence or in silent waiting. To suggest that you should spend two or three hours might sound incredible or even unbelievably boring. I admit that when I first heard about it, I was worried if I could keep still or maintain my focus for such a long period of time. As it was, I was re-assured that part of what makes a long Meeting distinct is that you can get up and move about during the worship.

I need not have worried. During the lunch, I sat next to a woman from Ireland who showed me the purple Quaker Life & Practice book from Ireland. It had simply not occurred to me that the red QF&P book that is quoted so often in British Quaker Meetings is actually only a British publication. Each different part of the world with Quakers has a different book of collected wisdom. The testimonies and the basic principles will be the same, but they will choose different ways of expressing it and different quotations to illustrate points. The next week I made sure to write to the Quaker HQ in Dublin and ask to buy a copy of the Irish book of Quaker Life. I recommend that anyone involved with Quakers does this - it is always worth remembering that our way of being a Quaker is not the same as other ways across the world.

This revelation was one I pondered once the Meeting took place. There was occasional spoken Ministry and the clock (which I was trying to ignore) ticked past an hour and some people needed to stretch their legs or leave the room briefly before returning. One theme that emerged several times was how God opens doors for us, only for us to spend a long time arguing why we could never go through the door, not realising that it is already open. My favourite Quaker quote is 'Live Adventurously' and I believe that that is a very important philosophy and possibly a contrast with some mainstream Christianity. God has given you talents for a reason, so you should go out into the world and use them. I think that shyness, fear, temptation and lethargy often stop us using our talents. We fear that the door is locked and that we will never have the energy to open it, but all we need to do is try the handle to find that it has been unlocked already.

As two hours approached, two people brought the Meeting to a close. This was quite a funny demonstration of just how much Quakers can improvise. It became clear that most of the Meeting had not felt that it was the right time to conclude and so a silence continued for around another half an hour with more Ministry. I would say do not try this in your local Meeting, but I have witnessed Meetings run on well over the hour when there is a lot to be said. If we believe that we are being inspired by the Spirit, then we need to remember that we cannot put a time limit on the Spirit either.

The next day I went back to Bull Street to the regular Meeting. I was glad that I did this, partly because the Renewal Meeting had taken place in an upper room, whereas the regular Meeting was in what was clearly a surviving original part of the building with rows of banked pews arranged around four sides of a square room. I was greeted warmly at the door and I explained who I was and where I came from.

In contrast to the day before, this was a mostly silent Meeting with only a little Ministry at the end from a Friend who had been delayed coming to Meeting and had used the chance to talk to someone of another denomination who was at the same tram stop. I do like the Quaker belief in talking to other denominations and finding what we have in common!

When we came to the notices at the end of the Meeting (this one was only an hour), I prepared to stand up to say who I was, which Meeting I came from and to convey my greetings to the Bull Street Meeting from Cardiff Meeting. I was not prepared for the woman reading the notices to say, "And we particularly welcome our visitor from Cardiff Meeting and ask him to return with our greetings". I suppose that there were only a small number of people there, but I can tell you that it is still impressive when someone has taken the trouble to remember who you are and where you are from after greeting you on the door.

It took me by surprise, but as you know by now, I have a fondness for Birmingham that is born out of surprise.

6. One Quaker and Simplicity

Earlier this year, my fridge freezer stopped working. This was annoying but not an immediate crisis as I had my other fridge. Perhaps I need to explain.

When I was married, we bought an American-style large fridge freezer. It was probably larger than was needed for two people, but it had a large fridge section and an equally large freezer. I was lucky enough to retain custody of it in the divorce and so moved it to my new home ... and found the problem that I had a large fridge freezer and a small kitchen. Luckily the previous occupants of the house had left their fridge behind, so the fridge freezer went in the shed.

To me, it is the height of sophistication to have an electricity supply in your shed. That tells you far more about me than sophistication. However, that was where the fridge freezer went and I filled the freezer with frozen food and used the fridge compartment when there was no room in the fridge in the kitchen. I referred to one as the Summer Fridge and the other as the Winter Fridge and on dark winter evenings, several friends became lost trying to make the difficult journey across the garden to the shed for ice cream.

That is why when I write that my fridge freezer broke down, there was no need for panic. I tried defrosting it, I tried all the instructions sent through by the manufacturers, but I had to face the fact that the freezer section was no longer freezing. The trouble was that if I wanted to buy a new freezer (I already had a fridge, remember), I would need to have the old fridge freezer removed and at that point another problem arose.

The only way to remove the broken fridge freezer would be through the back gates to the house. These back gates had become rotten and would not open. I was worried that removing the fridge freezer would end up with me losing the back gates in the process. Obviously they needed to be replaced first. It was time to call the carpenter.

Before this degenerates into a 'she swallowed the spider to catch the fly' type of tale, I should tell you that the exact nature of how to remove a fridge freezer from a shed, albeit an electric shed, is not important. The important part is people's reaction when I told them that I did not have a freezer. Due to the delay in buying the replacement - one month, two months, six months started to pass - what to some people sounded like an unfortunate situation caused by an appliance breakdown, now started to sound like a deliberate act of self-harm.

Yes, you should have heard the things that were said to me! 'How do you survive without a freezer?' was the basic question. After a while I started to be slightly cantankerous and ask the interrogator what they needed a fridge freezer for – with most consumer goods, you are not supposed to ask what something is for, you are just supposed to accept that you need it.

Let us take stock. I do not eat meat, so there was no need to freeze meat. I try to avoid convenience foods, so I had no need for freezing them. I try to make my own food and I would rather boil potatoes than cook chips. If I need peas in an instant, I could have them from a tin and not from a frozen packet (there seems to be a certain snobbery about tinned peas, but I can stand the snobbery). Every time someone told me what I needed a freezer for, I could explain to them why I did not need that item.

Frozen bread? Why do I need to freeze bread? If I need it I can buy it in the local shop next to the train station on the way home from work. Ice cream I admit sounded like a temptation but if it is supposed to be a treat, then why not leave it for buying at the seaside? I even had someone ask me what I would do for ice cubes. Ice cubes! There is no day of my life where I have woken up and thought 'you know, my life today will not be complete without ice cubes'.

What I thought would simply be a matter of living without a freezer for a while became an easy goal for me to accomplish and a challenge for other people. I think that some people genuinely felt that my ability to survive without a freezer was questioning and undermining their consumer choices. It was certainly making my electricity bill cheaper.

This, to me, is the core of the testimony around simplicity. People tend to think about it in terms of simple and non-extravagant dress codes and a rather austere approach to life. In fact, I think that in an economy driven by continuous consumption, it can be as easily aimed at asking what we need to survive. You should take a look around where you are living now and ask what exactly it is that you really need. Stop making excuses for most of it.

I have come to view Lent as a good opportunity to experiment with Quaker traditions. I know that there are plenty of Quakers who ignore Lent as just another one of those church festivals, but I have had some interesting sets of forty days and forty nights, including one where I tried to live a simple life. This was before the fridge freezer broke and so I now know that I should have switched that off as well, but bear with me.

Over the forty days, I tried to pare my life back to only things that I needed. I avoided using a car to drive anywhere, I only bought the food that I absolutely needed so that there was no waste and I took care not to spend on things that I did not need.

The result of this was a great deal of inconvenience. Travelling home from my evening classes by train meant that I was home nearly an hour later than I could have arrived home by car (the planet thanks you for your transport options). Cutting back on spending on luxuries did mean that I used a cheaper type of bubble bath and I avoided cakes and sweets. I did not go to the gym, but put on three layers of clothing if I went for a run outside. All these were doable, but annoying. However, one conversation stood out as saying much about consumerism.

I was in my local shop, buying a packet of four burger buns. I could use two for a meal that night and then keep the other two to make lunches with in the coming days. All fine and simple there. However, when I reached the till I was told to go back and take a second packet as they were 'two for one'. I only wanted one, I explained but I was told that they were two for one. No, I re-iterated, I only needed one packet of buns. The shop assistant moved from thinking that I was being stupid to thinking that I was being difficult and told me that I had to have the second packet. That was the offer – two for one, if you bought one you had to have the second. This was the point though, the 'bargain' mattered more than whether I needed the second packet or not. 'Getting the deal' had become the object of buying the buns rather than stopping my hunger for the night with a decent meal.

This is where I think that simplicity should speak most clearly to Quakers in the 21st century. We face lives that have been made intensely complex and untangling them will be hard. However, you should ask with everything if it is really about your need or about your convenience. If it is about your convenience, then are you being drawn into a situation like I was with the second packet of buns, where they would probably go mouldy and go to waste before I had a chance to use them? What excuses are you making in your life for things like the fridge freezer in the shed which you could actually live without? Be careful though, stepping away from consumer society will not bring you the approval of others.

Of course, you may have seen the irony of me writing the story about the freezer that I did not need and the buns that would go mouldy next to each other. I could have taken the extra packet of buns, if only i had had a freezer to put them in.

No-one said that simplicity was simple.

7. Caerleon Newport[15]

"A Society of Annes and Davids"

Poor Newport (South Wales) just cannot win. The first problem comes with the use of those brackets. If you have to mark yourself out as different to Newport (Isle of Wight), Newport (Pembrokeshire), Newport (Essex) and even Newport (Rhode Island), then you are probably going to have an identity problem. Believe you me, no-one sings about 'New York, New York' because they want to make sure you know which New York they are talking about.

Then there is the position. Newport's western boundaries bump up next to Cardiff's eastern boundaries. Drive between the two on the A48 and you will struggle to see where one starts and the other one ends. The result is that Newport tends to be overlooked in favour of its upstart neighbour. Upstart it is. It was Newport where the great Chartist rebellion of the 1830s took place, it was Newport that was the port and cradle for early industrialisation in Wales but along came Cardiff in the late nineteenth century to steal the glory. It is as though Newport had been an only child for years and then along came this crying baby that everyone suddenly fawned over.

---

[15] Since this chapter was written, Caerleon Newport has become Newport Meeting and found a new home. There will be an update in a future edition!

If you want an example, look at the NATO Summit held at Celtic Manor in 2014. This should have been a chance to 'put Newport on the map' as some of the world's most powerful leaders gathered in the city. Instead, media focus was on the leaders' evening meal in Cardiff. Even the Vale of Glamorgan tried to cash in on the event, with a big sign on the roundabout outside Cardiff airport saying 'Vale of Glamorgan Council Welcomes Barack Obama'.

I suppose that technically Caerleon is part of Newport but it is a different world. This is one reason why the Meeting name 'Caerleon Newport' intrigued me. I was curious to visit the Meeting there.

If Newport is the new port then Caerleon is the old port. It is site of very impressive Roman remains, one of the largest amphitheatres in the UK and a fine set of Roman baths. However, the Romans needed to fortify this area because of the years of fighting against the Britons who lived here. Caerleon lies over a bend in the river Usk, separated from the rest of Newport both physically and psychologically. It has historic sites, a town green and beautiful old pubs. If you want to see why there is the accusation that Quakers are only in white, middle-class areas then go to Caerleon.

I was relying on my own sense of navigation to find Caerleon. I had looked up the Meeting House location the night before (it was clearly in a rented space on 'Church Street') but I decided that I had could leave the M4 at Junction 26 and find my way on my own from there. That was a big mistake. I was soon heading north and clearly going in the wrong direction. I turned around and discovered that I had to drive through Newport itself to find the turning for Caerleon. There was a traffic jam – at ten in the morning on a Sunday? – and I was starting to become a little stressed that I was not going to make the start of the Meeting, let alone arrive with enough time to talk to people and find out a little more about their Meeting.

As I headed out from the city centre on a dual carriageway, I saw a sign for Caerleon and tried to work out if it was a right turn or straight ahead. I took slightly too long to look at it and when my eyes returned to the road, a car in front had done an emergency stop and had its hazard lights on straight in front of me. I looked over my right shoulder and thankfully there was no-one there, so I was able to swerve around the car. However, it would only have taken the learner driver who was slightly behind on my right to have been further forwards and I would have been choosing which of the two cars to hit.

There are times when we all need to calm down and remember that we are part of a bigger plan. It may not seem like it and the machinations of our daily life probably seem too trivial to concern a Higher Power, but I am convinced that we should be more trusting and less panicked about what we are doing. That is not to say that we should be passive – on the contrary, the Spirit calls us to activity, not passivity- but that we need to trust more in the Spirit and less in ourselves. Yes, I avoided hitting the car but it did not matter because I was at the Meeting with ten minutes to spare. I need not have bothered with the panic.

Caerleon Newport Meeting takes place (at the time of writing) in the community centre on Church Street. I am glad that I looked it up the night before as there were no signs to advertise it and I was not sure that the door was unlocked when I arrived. This is one of the troubles with hired spaces and the lack of signage can be problem for the newcomer.

There was no doubt about the welcome once I arrived, I was shown into the Meeting room where a small group of

Friends chatted to me enthusiastically about Quakerism in the area. It seemed as though the Meeting in Caerleon owed its existence to a Friend from Cardiff who had decided to establish a Meeting there some years previously. It was only an occasional Meeting – first and third Sundays only.

It started in a house. I think that sometimes we forget that our Meeting Houses can be just that, houses. For all that churches are called the 'house of God', is the point that we make that God can be in all of our houses, not just the ones with a pointy roof?

The community centre was an example of this in its own way. The room was a 'Memorial Hall' proudly displaying the 'roll of honour' for those who died in the two world wars. I have no issue with honouring the dead, but I wondered how the owners of the centre would feel if I asked for a roll of honour for conscientious objectors or those who died supporting the war effort in non-combative roles? The large sign next to the plaques that warned that no food and drink could be consumed in the room probably told me the answer to that question. This was a place that liked rules and joining a small group of Quakers for tea and biscuits after Meeting was going to be an act of rebellion of its own kind.

You might note that I was greeted in the Meeting room. This was an innovation that I had not encountered before. I remember that in Bath there was an entrance area that was part of the Meeting room, but it was definitely screened off from the room itself. Here we were standing on the edge of the circle of chairs having the usual discussion before Meeting started. It was interesting.

I asked about this and I was told that it had come about as a result of a Meeting with the Kindlers where they asked what impression was given to newcomers arriving at the building. I should point out for non-Quaker readers that the Kindlers are not a group of people who spend a lot of time reading e-books on portable devices. I could pretend that I know all about them through some judicious later editing, but at the time of the conversation I only knew that they were a Quaker group who were mentioned regularly.

I do quite like keeping the circle of chairs 'sacred' in the sense that the Meeting starts when the first person sits down and those who wish to talk can do so outside the Meeting room. However, there was also an immediacy to this arrangement that meant that when I did come to sit down, I already felt part of a supportive group.

A candle flickered on the table in the middle and I started to concentrate on the silence. After a while there was Ministry about some of the notable dates and achievements in Quaker history. My mind was drawn towards the section of Quaker Faith & Practice which warns against looking only successes and not failures too but I decided not to say anything because when the speaker reached '1963 : The publication 'Towards a Quaker View of Sex' recognises that same sex relationships have the same validity as opposite sex relationships' the woman sitting next to me muttered, '1963 – wow'. It felt better to leave the 'wow' in those dates rather than immediately start talking about where we had not succeeded.

I have to tell you that I had one of the deepest experiences of silent worship that I had had for some time. I heard a clock outside strike eleven and soon afterwards found myself totally overtaken by a thought. It was not a sleep and it was not meditation, it just felt like my mind was totally occupied, but in a calming way. It ended when I heard the clock outside strike eleven fifteen and I was convinced that it had only been a minute since it struck eleven.

It can be hard to explain this kind of feeling but afterwards I felt totally refreshed and full of energy. It was as if I had sat there with my palms held open waiting for what tools I needed to make it through the day and they had been given to me.

I have had that experience before but it had not happened for a while before I visited Caerleon. I wondered if this was because I have been an Elder[16] in my home Meeting for the last ten months and even before then I had responsibilities or worries about who was attending and who was not attending. In other words, in a Meeting where you have responsibilities, your mind always has something to distract it from the silence but in a Meeting where you have no such distractions, it can be easier to reach the point of complete immersion in the worship[17].

After the Meeting we had tea and biscuits (in direct contravention of the community centre rules). This was indeed a point that was raised in the discussions. The Meeting was actively looking for new premises to hire and many of the points that I had made were echoed. They wanted to engage more with Newport, they wanted to have a space where they could have tea and biscuits without breaking the rules and so on. They did have a room with a wonderful glass wall which let light flood the

---

[16] Have I explained Elders yet? We may not have a hierarchy, but people do serve for three years at a time in a rotating organisational role. Sometimes this leads to Elders spending their worship time thinking about the organisation that needs doing.

[17] Is it really worship someone asked me once. Yes was my reply - everything is worship, even writing songs about courgettes ... see the chapter on creativity!

Meeting and the location did have its advantages, but a committee had been looking at alternative venues.

It was at this point that the principle of 'discernment' really came into its own. There were four 5th Sundays during the next year and so it was proposed that an extra Meeting be added to the calendar for each 5th Sunday, to take place in one of the four locations shortlisted by the buildings committee. By the end of the year, they would have experienced all the potential new locations and would be able to discern if the Spirit had led them to favour a particular one.

Naturally it would be a slow process, but it was better to take time to identify the guidance of the Spirit than to have a contentious debate, a vote or leave it in the hands of a committee. I think that anyone interested in how discernment works could take that as an excellent example.

I was introduced to a lot of people named Anne and a lot of people named David. For a moment I thought that this summed up the Religious Society of Friends – it is a Society of Annes and Davids. At first glance, we do look like the white, middle-class warriors of the religious world sometimes. The suggestion that comes with it is that we are actually the comfortably off worriers of the religious world. Quakers are very aware of this and although I am not sure that I have heard any definite solutions on how to broaden our appeal as Meetings, it is something that I hear discussed often.

Yet, I think that sometimes it is our very stillness that fools people. The Quakers arrested at fracking sites or arms fayres and indeed those who pray for them each Sunday are acting in a way that puts their comfortably off life in jeopardy. Annes and Davids can 'talk truth to power' too.

I hope that the Quakers of Caerleon Newport are guided to find a new home where they can expand their membership and reach new areas. Towards the end of the Meeting, the candle on the central table started to flicker as if it were just about to go out. At that moment, a brilliant burst of sunlight from outside the room fell across the library table, through the gathered circle and on to the table itself. The light is always shining from somewhere.

8. One Quaker and Equality

I think that Equality is the hardest of all the Quaker testimonies. It is a little deceptive in that regard. Truth should be difficult because so much of our lives are based around subtle of not so subtle deceptions or untruths (see the chapter on truth), simplicity should challenge us all to give up some of the luxuries that we expect as part of our lifestyles (see the chapter on simplicity) and pacifism is a hard thing to stand up for in a threatening and confrontational world (see ... you know it by now). However, take my word for it, if there were a fight, equality would emerge as harder than pacifism, but that would probably be because pacifism would refuse to fight.

Everyone likes to think that they believe in equality. You will hear plenty of people saying that they treat everyone equally and no-one saying 'the thing about me is, I like to treat people unequally'. Plenty of people will tell you that life is not fair, but few people will say that they do not treat other people fairly. There are many (Quakers and non-Quakers alike) who will tell you that the real commitment should be to **equity**. I like the explanation of the difference to be that equality means that everyone receives the same slice of the cake, equity means that the hungriest receive a bigger slice than those who are full.

Yet, I suspect that equality may also be Christianity's greatest gift to civilisation. Paying lip service to equality or equity is easy, putting it in to practice can be a lot harder. Let me start by explaining one of the profound reflections I had while in my early Quaker days and how it framed how I thought of equality from then on.

I was having my lunch in the Wales Millennium Centre in Cardiff Bay. There was an area of comfortable seating around a stage in the public area of the Centre and as I worked nearby, I would often sit there and eat my lunch whether there was a performance on stage or not. On this occasion, there was not. Behind me were a couple of men talking business, to my left was the seating area for a coffee shop where a waitress was tidying up plates and in the bar next door some BBC employees were exchanging plans for a new series (it is where the BBC Wales employees go to talk about props or staging). After my lunch, I fell asleep. It was quite a warm day and I was tired and relaxed, so drifted off for a few minutes. As I awoke, the reflection struck me that each of those people – the businessmen, the waitress, the BBC employees and me – all had exactly the same opportunity to speak the word of God. When it came to the Spirit, all of them could be used to give lessons or thoughts or ideas to the world. In that same second I realised how completely against the ordering of our society that reflection was. We value business and men more than we value art and women. We value people who work for the BBC more than we value waitresses. We probably also value people who do not fall asleep after eating their lunch more than those who do, but that one may just be good business sense rather than prejudice. Everything around us is hierarchical and yet the Quaker call to equality is a challenge to that. No-one is better than you. You are better than no-one.

I write 'Quaker' but the basic value of every human being is there in Christ's teaching, it is just that churches based on hierarchies can seem not to be emphasising it. Indeed, one might say that Quakers sometimes forget to emphasise it too. At one of my first Area Meetings, I found myself in a discussion of Eldership and Oversight. A woman from another Meeting asked me what I knew about the subject and when she had decided that I did not know as much as she did, she proceeded to lecture me about why Quakers did not have a hierarchy of priests. I pondered that her patronising attitude was an attempt to set up such a hierarchy among our discussion group.

You might say that we have all been guilty of this from time to time. My Meeting would not be alone in occasionally referring to 'weighty Quakers', meaning those in the Meeting who were known to give good Ministry or could be relied upon to talk well of Quakers at a gathering with non-Quakers. There are no 'weighty Quakers', there are only Quakers surely? We have no priesthood – or rather every Quaker is a priest – but are we so sure that our own Meetings really have no-one considered better than others?

However, this is only in a religious sense so far. Start to expand it to the whole of society and you see just what a challenge it is. We are all aware of the language of division and hatred that exists around immigrants, Muslims, single mothers ... you name whoever is in the firing line currently. I am sure that Quakers probably also think about gender equality and sexuality equality too. There are some remarkable tales from the seventeenth and eighteenth century of the surprise of many at the way some Quaker marriages were run as if the woman and man involved were equal.

We should think about equality as about more than 'issues' or discrimination though. That person down the road from you who has bought a bright purple sofa which you want to tell them looks tacky (to you) – they are your equal. The person who struggles to grasp your joke and you think that they are dull for it – they are your equal. The person in your workplace who gets all the promotions even though you think that they do not have the talent – they are your equal. Next time you watch a reality TV show and you are tempted to look down on the performers or when you see a quiz show and want to mock the intelligence of the competitors – they are your equal.

I would recommend that you pause tomorrow (it is too late today) and listen to how you talk about other people. Are you seeing that of God in all of them? More than that, are you accepting them all as your equal and a vessel for the Spirit as much as you are? I would say that if your answer is an unequivocal 'yes' then you are not listening to yourself carefully enough. When you are next having a conversation with someone you do not like, listen for all the things that you tell yourself that show that you are superior to them and then realise how wrong you are.

Yes, it is a challenge in the extreme cases – I had great admiration for the Archbishop of Canterbury Rowan Williams when he spoke about being troubled by the shooting of an unarmed man when Osama Bin Laden was killed. I knew that there would be protests in the USA and claims that Williams was 'siding with terrorists'. However, I thought that he was right. Hard as it is to accept, there was that of God in Osama Bin Laden, though clearly his actions did not follow what the Spirit was telling him. I have had a Quaker in my Meeting advocate clearly that those who have travelled to the Middle East to fight with ISIS should be arrested and executed on their return to the UK. Some might agree, but I find it hard to see the testimony to equality in revenge.

At this point, plenty of people plead 'but I am better than that person down the road – my taste in home furnishings is different, I do behave better in front of my children, I have never become involved in a street altercation with my neighbour over where they park their car'. I am saying that the call to equality calls us to forget all our attempts to believe that we are better than anyone else. We all have that of God in us and we are all capable of being messengers of the Spirit. Instead of criticising one another, we should concentrate on hearing that message and acting on it every day. There should be no time to look down on others.

I recommend that you go into any packed area and look at the human beings there for a second. You will have all sorts of thoughts and judgements about who they are, what status they have in our society and what they are doing. Now imagine that everything that you think about them is wrong and they are simply waiting for the call of the Spirit ... they are no different to you. They are your equal. I think that if that does not strike you as the hardest testimony of them all, you should continue looking at them until it does (though please avoid staring).

9. Basingstoke

"Mysterious Ways"

It is always an awkward question to ask. If you are staying with someone for the weekend, it is not always straightforward to say that you want to disappear on a Sunday morning to find their local Quaker Meeting, especially if this is the first time that they have heard that you are a Quaker. 'What is a Quaker?' and 'What do Quakers believe?' normally follow. If you are reading these chapters in order, then you will know that my first introduction to travelling as a Quaker came because the friend I was staying with mentioned going to the local Meeting House. It is harder when you decide in advance that you want to go to a Meeting while a guest of a friend.

I had already put out Steve and his family[18] by turning up during the Lent when I was trying to live as a vegan for forty days and nights. He was very generous about standing in the supermarket while I pondered what products had had milk slipped into them without anyone noticing (bread is a surprise offender – bread! You do not need milk in bread!). However, generosity usually indicates an open mind and I was happy to tell both Steve and his wife that I was interested in visiting the Basingstoke Meeting on Sunday morning and that I had its location and details from the Quaker website.[19]

---

[18] Not necessarily his real name but his real family

[19] Always look up the Meeting House on StreetView in advance too – they all look different and it will help if you have seen a picture of it first

I attempted to give a potted history of Quakerism and probably left out as much as I left out when trying to explain the subject earlier in this book. When I mentioned that some Quakers in the USA were executed for being Quakers but that that the persecution had been less violent in the UK, Steve's wife noted that Quakers in the UK had fared better than Roman Catholics then. It is a fair point and a useful reminder that we should never claim a monopoly on persecution.

We arrived at Sunday morning without drama - even surviving a Saturday night where I insisted on telling people who were drinking beer that their drink had been filtered through fish intestines (that one seems like a no-brainer to me, vegan or carnivore. We can make beer by draining it through fish intestines or we can make beer without draining it through fish intestines, why would we keep doing it?). Steve asked if he could come along to the meeting and I was simultaneously pleased and a little bit worried about how the Quaker world would present itself.

Basingstoke's Meeting House was in the southern area of the city and we found it without too much difficulty. It was another one which was genuinely a house and I found out later that the upstairs was a privately-rented flat with only the downstairs given over to Quaker pursuits.

One thing I have noticed is that Quaker Meetings are perpetually half full (not half empty, we are not pessimists). Almost every time I visit a new one, I am told 'oh, there are a lot of people at regional meeting' or 'the usual clerk is not here' or some other reason why some people are missing. I think that this is just modesty about who we are but really we ought to say that each week as many of the people whom the Spirit wishes to gather have gathered and the Meeting is therefore not half full but completely full of those who should be there.

The Meeting Room was in the front room of the house – much like the arrangement in Portsmouth – and we were greeted in the corridor outside with the explanation that there were a lot of the regular people missing. We were then shown into the meeting room and took our seats in a group of seven or eight people.

The Meeting was entirely silent and this was to have a lasting effect on me. It is not that I have anything against silent Meetings – I have been to many and they can be very powerful – but this was the first time that I had thought about them from an outsider's point of view. When you take a visitor to a Quaker Meeting, you do spend some time wondering what they are making of this rather unusual form of worship.

After the Worship[20] both Steve and I chatted to those present. As ever, it was interesting to hear the stories of the Meeting, a little of its history and the details of the lodger who lived upstairs and who could occasionally be heard[21].

I started to ask myself what Steve had learned about Quakers. On the one hand, he must have come away with the idea that we are friendly and welcoming to strangers. I had also pointed out to him the sign on the Meeting room window which said, "Thou Shalt Decide For Yourselves". Clearly it was a way of being which relied on individual understanding, then. There were posters around the Meeting room about protecting the

---

[20] We call the 'silent' part of the Meeting 'worship'. Personally, I find the chatting around tea and biscuits afterwards a valuable part of Meeting too and its own form of Worship. I use a capital letter for Worship for no particular reason.

[21] 'Be still for the presence of the Lord is moving in this place' – though, joking aside, you will note that I never use the word 'Lord'. That is for a particular reason.

environment, ending greed, being a Quaker as part of your identity and working for peace through co-operation. I always remark to myself that Quakers do good posters.

However, there was nothing in the Worship that said who we are, what we believe or even how our way of being works. This is the problem with 'the gathered Meeting'. Once you understand it and are part of it, then it does make sense and you can value the silence and the waiting on the Spirit. It is harder as an outsider to appreciate what is going on and not think about whether people elsewhere in the circle are making a laundry list or other mundane tasks to pass the time. I do have an answer to that question, but I will come back to it.

In Cardiff, we have started (or re-started) a tradition of reading from Quaker Faith & Practice every month. An Elder is asked to take responsibility for this each month and he or she will approach others in the Meeting to ask if they would bear in mind a chapter of QF&P and see if the Spirit calls them to read a particular passage.

This can be very effective. One month I was asked to read from QF&P should the Meeting proceed in silence. We had had forty minutes of silence one Sunday and I was starting to feel as though a reading was needed. I flicked through QF&P and found a couple of passages that seemed relevant. I was in two minds about them, but I felt called to read them out so stood and read both short paragraphs.

After I had done this, I had about five minutes of self-doubt where I wondered if I had chosen correctly. I wondered if I should have spoken at all. This is not uncommon, by the way. People think of religions based on the individual as being full of wannabe street preachers declaring their own view of God with great confidence. I have met many Quakers who say that after speaking in

Meeting they are overcome with doubt and worry about whether that was what they should have done. This can be a very good check on ego.

Before I was able to be too filled with self-doubt, a man on the other side of the circle stood up and said how much he had needed to hear both the passages that I had read. He related them to his own experience and then sat down. He was followed by someone who gave their thoughts around the subject and so on until the last fifteen minutes of the Meeting had been filled with thought-provoking Ministry. That, I thought, is the power of being called to break the silence.

Are people putting together their laundry list in the silence? Maybe they are. We do have leaflets for people attending their first Meeting that explain what they are all about, but it must seem strange. I have fallen asleep more than a few times. I was once at a Quaker conference where someone asked if anyone had fallen asleep in Meeting and there was a slow acceptance around the table that everyone had done it at least once. I take it as the Spirit telling me that I need to rest.

However, I think that this is okay. There will be Meetings where you become very deeply aware of the silence and the spirituality of the moment and there will be Meetings where you never seem to settle. I think that it takes time to become used to all this and I wonder if sometimes we lose people after a few visits because they are not 'getting it'.

I walked back through Basingstoke with Steve. He had enjoyed the experience but was not sure quite what to make of the silence and found it hard to quite get a handle on Quakers with so little information about worship to go on. This was fair enough. As we walked back to his house, he did reflect though that the silence had given him valuable time to consider how to organise the coming week and which tasks he had to do and when and so it had been valuable. I smiled to myself because in that comment I heard the Spirit having been part of his life too. If you come away from Meeting with your life more organised, you should not assume that you were distracted from what you were supposed to hear.

10. One Quaker and the Quakers of the Internet

Every now and then in Meeting, I have mentioned that I am part of a number of online groups which discuss religion, spirituality and Quakers. Sometimes I allude to disputes and discussions among them and I know that many people will nod their head and think that this sounds typical of online discussions.

A Friend came up to me after one piece of Ministry where I had mentioned the internet and asked about some of these arguments.

"Even Quakers can be unpleasant online," I replied.

He gave me a scathing look and I knew immediately what he was picking up on. The tendency to talk about 'even Quakers' as if they are a breed apart from other human-beings is not a good one. Quakers are human and just as capable of getting into pointless 'flame wars' online as anyone else. Perhaps the question is whether they should do and what (if anything) is in the Quaker testimonies which might suggest that Quakers should have a different approach to online debate to the approach taken by other people.

I had been thinking about the internet before this. I have a busy life and there is something very frustrating about checking an internet discussion group and finding something that requires a long answer which you do not have time to write. Worse still is when someone has mistaken your words or accused you of something and you want to have the time to reply. I had increasingly found myself posting in a thread once and then either not checking back on it or only checking back on it when I had time. So that I did not look rude, I often ended my contribution with a note that once I had made my contribution, I did not intend to make any other on the subject.

In time, I started to realise that this 'one contribution per thread' discipline was very useful. It helped me focus my thoughts in one concise piece and stopped me being drawn into long discussions that were not going anywhere. In fact, when I thought about it, it reminded me of the discipline of Meeting because it meant not speaking twice and not responding to previous Ministry directly.[22]

In fact, I have seen this principle applied to (offline) Quaker discussion groups. 'Worship sharing' is asked for, where each person shares their reaction to something and no-one is allowed to speak twice or directly answer a point until everyone has had a chance to share something. If that sounds tedious, I recommend trying the other kind of discussion with a more critical eye. I was once in a discussion on pacifism and I realised that under normal discussion rules, two particularly forthright people would argue for an hour and steamroller others out of the conversation. If Quakers value everyone's contribution, then worship sharing is a way of being inclusive.

I once said this to a group of Quaker Friends and one replied with the suggestion that worship sharing stopped 'healthy discussion'. I disagree and I wonder how much 'normal' discussion is actually healthy. If I go to a discussion group where worship sharing is to be used, I

[22] For those not familiar with it, this is the discipline of Meeting – you make one contribution and do not use it to discuss what has just been said, although you may say that you have been prompted by someone else's words to think more on a subject.

feel immensely relieved and also valued. If there is that of God in everyone, then there should be equal opportunity for everyone to express the divine.

At first, I thought that I was being needlessly sensitive about internet discussions. They are famed for descending into pointless arguments, why should I care? I suppose that I was looking for Quakers to have a higher standard. It was not a case of 'even Quakers' but that just as we say that what you say on Sunday should be what you do on Monday, then what you do offline should be what you do online too.

Not long after this, I posted a comment about Iran on a Quaker Group. I was making a more general point, but I referred to Iran as a theocracy. This was lazy typing as I know that Iran is a more complicated society than that. I know this from a variety of sources. I have friends (and a Friend) who have been to Iran, I have read about the country and I have a good understanding of politics. I am not an expert, but I am also not someone who is making snap judgements about a country.

A fellow Quaker took issue with my comments and added, "You shouldn't believe everything you read in the mainstream media." This interested me. He was assuming that I was being naive or ignorant because (presumably unlike him) I did not have a range of sources for my ideas. He seemed not to have considered that I might have been lazy rather than ill-informed.

The key point in that reaction is 'presumably unlike him'. The phrasing of the response suggests to me that the person who wrote it believed and wanted to prove to other people that he was superior to me. This is a typical comment from a discussion in its normal sense – as part of 'winning' the argument, you must prove yourself superior to the other person. Surely though, if we believe in equality, if we believe in that of God in everyone, if we believe in discerning the will of the Spirit, then there should be no 'winning' and no attempts to prove personal superiority?

I posted to one of the (online) Quaker discussion groups a rather tongue-in-cheek question. I started with what I thought was an extravagantly-phrased thought, 'I am starting to think that Quakers should not post on the internet'. Perhaps the response proved my point as some people took this very seriously and thought that I was advocating a Quaker boycott of the internet. I continued by asking whether you should be thoughtful about what you post and how you come across online if you are a Quaker.

The immediate answer from some people was 'no'. Indeed, someone noted that it was not Ministry. This intrigued me as I had always thought that everything that you said or wrote should pass the same test as Ministry in a Meeting. I persisted and now began to realise that the principle of contributing once to a discussion and then not contributing again was a good discipline too. Only being able to contribute once does focus your thoughts and challenges you to say what you have to say in the simplest manner possible.

What were the reactions to this? One person haughtily told me, "Good – it means you might listen more than you talk". Given that I contribute to that Group only once in a blue moon, this was both inaccurate and annoying. Then again, what was she saying? Ah yes, that my contributions were not as valued as hers. So much of human discussion is focussed not on issues but trying to prove yourself superior.

Should we do better? I genuinely believe that as Quakers we can do. I think that the internet will remain a Wild

West of discussion where people will be rude, obnoxious, threaten to kill people and give the impression of a group of people standing in a field shouting very loudly. Then again, society has plenty of people who are rude and obnoxious. I admit that threatening to kill people tends to occur more online, but if you think that people do not shout at each loudly then try driving during rush hour. We are called upon as Quakers to 'be patterns and examples' and just as we should be examples of a simpler, more honest, more equal and less confrontational way of living offline, so we should have those values online. Our best evangelism offline is when people ask 'why are you such a peaceful [or other value] person?' and we can reply 'because I am a Quaker'. That intrigues people so much more than when a stranger jumps in front of them in the street and yells, 'You should be a Quaker! It's so much fun!'.

Why not take these principles online? Why not stand apart from those who seek to confront and divide online? Why not be patterns and examples in the online world too? 'This is not Ministry' was one person's objection – but why should any part of your life not be Ministry?

11. Swansea

"Weathering the Storm"

I went to Swansea Meeting at the end of a heatwave. This was not just the end of any heatwave mind you, it was the end of a prolonged period of hot weather where I had become accustomed to wearing shorts and sandals and expecting each day to be sunny and bright. The end of the heatwave seemed just as extreme with sudden heavy showers moving in and the wind blowing everything away. It was as if we were caught between two extremes and it was easy to take seriously the joke in a MAD magazine article about giving up hope – "Two of the leading causes of death on this planet are floods and drought. One happens when it rains, the other happens when it doesn't."

Swansea is one of the most visible Quaker Meeting Houses that I have seen. I was told that the impressive Victorian structure in central Swansea with 1888 carved into its stonework has only been a Meeting House for around fifty years, but it looks as though it was designed for the purpose. It stands at one end of the Kingsway, one of Swansea's central streets and until very recently the scene of some of its most boisterous nightlife. Although buildings further down the street have been demolished and replaced with nondescript steel and glass office blocks, the Meeting House was presumably once a large family home and its large bay window and front garden do look a little out of place. Then again, any building with 'Quaker Meeting House' in large lettering on its front is going to look out of place.

I used to work in Swansea before I was a Quaker, but I remember seeing the building quite often. It is near Swansea's central mosque but whereas I had been on a tour of the mosque and had an explanation of what goes on inside it, the Meeting House had remained a mystery. However, it is one of the most visible Meeting Houses that I know, so its presence at the end of Kingsway had been unmissable.

The weather was pretty terrible on the day that I went to Swansea Meeting. I had arrived early and thought about a walk around the local area but what with the rain and the building work in Swansea at the time, it seemed as though the Meeting House would at least be a dry oasis.

At this point in my travels, I was coming close to having been to twenty different Meetings and so I was starting to become familiar with different practices. Now I look for who is the doorkeeper and what kind of welcome they give you. I wonder who will spot that I am a newcomer and approach me for conversation. Most of all, now that I am serving as an Elder of Cardiff Meeting, I look at whether I can spot who the Elders of the Meeting are[23].

In some Meetings you have a sense of who is leading things without having to look too far. Sometimes they all sit in the centre of the circle. I have even seen one Meeting with a raised section of chairs, though they did assure me that that was historic and that they embraced

---

[23] Each Meeting has a group of Elders who look after the running of the Meeting. They are appointed for three years only, so that there is never a permanent hierarchy and responsibility rotates around the members of that Meeting. An Elder will typically be the person who stands up at the end of the Meeting and tells everyone what is going on that day or Quaker activities in the week. They will probably talk to you if you are a newcomer.

the equality of everyone sitting at the same level now. I like Meetings such as Swansea where I can join the circle of chairs and not know who is an Elder and who is not.

Where Quakers meet has long been a subject of interest to me. Anyone with a sense of mischief can suggest that the solution to Cardiff Meeting House's troubles would be to sell the building in the city centre location and move to a new build on an industrial estate on the edge of the city. You can imagine how unpopular this idea is and yet it does raise a question – if Quaker buildings are in city centres, is that for a reason other than ease of travel for their worshippers?

Do Quakers do 'outreach'? It is hard to say. Some Quakers believe that we should be leafleting (as Quakers did very seriously in their early days) and going out and talking to people about our faith. Other Quakers believe that their role is to pray quietly for others to be guided to Quaker ways. There are also those who believe that they should try to live a good life and that this will inspire others to find out more about Quakers. They are all a part of the Quaker experience I would argue, but without being visible, are Quakers invisible? Furthermore, does visibility mean anything without acting on it? I saw the Meeting House in Swansea for years before I ever went in it. It was visible, just not part of the life that I was leading[24].

Personally, I would like to see Quakers do more to be visible, though I suspect that many will fear that this means jumping out at people on Kingsway and saying 'Look at me, I'm a Quaker!' Hopefully we could be more subtle than that. How else will people know who we are and what we stand for?

---

[24] If you are reading this book in the regular order, then you will already have read 'One Quaker and Invisibility', which is a longer discussion of outreach.

I once said that if I had advice for my younger self, it would be 'never discount the role that Swansea will play in your life'. I have never lived in the city and yet it keeps playing a prominent part in my journey. I did my teacher training in Swansea, I asked my ex-wife to marry me in Swansea (that was before she was my ex-wife, of course), I had my favourite job in Swansea between 2005 and 2009 before I was made redundant, I dated a woman who I went to a salsa class with in Swansea ... you name it, if it is going to happen, it is going to happen in Swansea.

If it sounds as though this is more about survival than achievement then I would agree. There is a degree to which I feel as though I have weathered a storm and, in our own way, so have Quakers. There is an understandable and constant worry about the decline in membership of the Religious Society of Friends just as there is any religious organisation in 21st century Britain. We are no longer persecuted as we were in the seventeenth century but dare I suggest that persecution at least meant that someone took notice of us? Is the question now whether we are relevant anymore?

This brings me back to Swansea Meeting. It was as lovely and friendly as you would expect if you have been reading carefully and there was interesting Ministry and a good cup of tea on offer. However, whereas I knew everything about the Mosque when I was working in Swansea, I knew nothing of the Quaker Meeting. There is always a balance to be struck between tradition and innovation and Quakers have sometimes been leaders of change and sometimes taken time to catch up with change. This should not be surprising. When in Swansea, I was also reminded of how even in an open and inclusive society, rituals are established that bond insiders and can exclude outsiders.

I have probably mentioned at some point in this book that at the end of a Quaker Meeting, everyone shakes hands. Those from the Anglican tradition will recognise this as a 'sign of peace' and I was once very glad to shake the hand of a man who had disagreed with me profoundly throughout a discussion group – the act is one of equals re-affirming their equality.

However, I am so used to doing it that I forget that it is not as commonplace as I had thought that it was. At the end of the Meeting in Swansea, there was no shaking of hands, but people stood in a circle and held hands. However, there was no indication that this was going to happen and for the inexperienced newcomer, it could be confusing. The symbolism is the same, I suppose, it re-affirms the joined and equal nature of the participants, but if you are not aware that it is coming, then you risk breaking the circle.

Sometimes I wonder how well Quakers adapt to changing times. One of the most obvious examples of this to me is paper. Quakers, despite their environmental commitments, seem to use a lot of paper. In my local Meeting, we have a membership book printed on paper, an area magazine printed on paper, a national magazine printed on paper ... and none of these things is available in e-format.

I know this because at one point I suggested that the membership book should be an e-copy with people having to ask specially to have a paper copy. At the time we were printing about sixty copies of this membership book per year but finding that only half of them were taken by people. The most common objection to this that I heard was 'what about people who want it on paper?' Each time I explained that things would still be available on paper but people would have to ask for them, but still people assumed that e-copies were going to replace paper.

I know that this probably reads as unfair to those who are used to having things on paper or who are not confident with technology. This is a fair point. However, I saw the gap between how the Meeting operated and the expectations of younger members when I talked to someone who was in their twenties about having their name in the membership book. I had to explain that to do this she would have to fill in a consent form and post it to someone who collated these and who would then add her name to the list. She looked at me with incredulity and replied, "You want me to post it?"

I started by writing about how I walked into the heatwave dressed in a t-shirt, shorts and sandals. I wonder if sometimes this is how we behave as Quakers. Perhaps no-one is ever really prepared for what is coming and perhaps that is the point. After the storm has passed, the wind has died down and the rain has stopped, the Quaker Meeting House will still be standing there ready to welcome people in. We have been through worse.

12. One Quaker and Being Prepared

One thing that may come across in this book is how different each Quaker Meeting is. I suppose that you could say that churches and chapels are all different, not to mention synagogues or mosques, but there seems something particularly diverse about Quaker Meeting Houses. It is probably to do with their history and to do with the Society's general aversion to formality and procedure. I have read that when the commission for building Friends House[25] in London was drawn up, it was a deliberate in-joke to ask interested architects to build 'in the Quaker style'.

Some things are reasonably common, however. Most Meetings seem to have a circular formulation to their seating. This makes sense as it is an echo of the 'round table' idea of equality. There are no 'leaders' to sit at the front and tell you what to do, we can all learn from one another. In the middle there is often a table and that table may have books, plants or – especially in Scandinavian Quaker circles I am told - a candle. People have done research studies on what Quakers put on their central table and this has created reactions running from 'why does it matter?' to 'of course, you could not put that there!' I was at a Meeting at the Quaker Study Centre in Woodbroke where someone brought in a branch that had fallen from a tree and placed it on the central table.

[25] The closest thing we have to a Quaker HQ is Friends House in Euston. They co-ordinate campaigns, press and other functions ... though as you might imagine individual Quaker Meetings will take their own stance on things. See Chapter 22.

However, when someone asks 'what happens in a Quaker Meeting?', there are a wide range of answers. No two Meetings are the same and no two meetings of a Meeting are the same - just because it happened that way in Cardiff this Sunday, it does not mean that it will happen the same way next Sunday. This can cause confusion, especially for newcomers or those who are Quaker-curious. This is where people start to ask if it might not be a good guide for people to prepare something to say in advance.

Welcome Friends and friends to the controversial world of Prepared Ministry.

It is hard to underestimate the heat levels that this topic has produced in some places I have been and in some online discussions that I have witnessed. It is a particular bugbear online because it helps to explain the differences between UK Meetings and Meetings in the USA. However, if you have taken on board that Quaker Meetings happen in silence unless someone is inspired to speak, you may ask if people start to pre-empt the Spirit by thinking of things to say in advance.

Whoever said that silence is golden may well have been right in terms of its value and rarity, but it is also threatening. We live in a world of noise and activity and so silent waiting stands at the opposite of the tone and tenor of modern living. Why else is it significant that we stand in silence when remembering tragic events? Indeed, if you have ever heard a minute's silence held in a football ground, you will be struck by how its power is in the contrast with the noise made by twenty thousand fans cheering once it is over.

I will admit that it is also one of the reasons that I go to Quaker Meetings. In a weekend, I might spend 48 hours being busy, rushing around and generally running from one thing to another. An hour's quiet and stillness is a contrast to all that. Indeed, there are those who object to using the name 'worship' for this because that implies more activity (and praise) and this may lead people to expect something different from Quaker worship.

You are all quiet and wait on the Spirit to inspire someone, but what if that does not happen? It sounds as though it would be boring, but there is a great spiritual depth to be found in an hour's silence. We are wrong to assume that a silence means that nothing is happening. In fact, I wonder how many people would be able to be truly still and thoughtful for an hour without some practice? I will happily admit that some times I have fallen asleep in Meeting, but I always think that that may be a sign that I need the rest even more than I had realised.

However, for those who do not like an hour of silence, the question has to be what you do about it? Some people believe that you should plan a reading or a statement for each week so that there is something happening. Anything that is worked out in advance in that way is known as 'prepared ministry' and it is frowned on by many because it is not directly inspired by the Spirit during a Meeting.

In Cardiff, there was quite a long debate about this. The proposal was that someone should take responsibility each month for making a reading from Quaker Faith & Practice if there had been no other Ministry after a 'significant time' (not agreed upon what that meant). Sometimes this might prompt people to give other comments on a theme or it might encourage reaction or development. I was put in charge of this one month and this did cause one particularly odd incident. I made a reading from QF&P about generosity and there were people who spoke after me. Towards the end of the hour, someone who had come in late and missed the original reading, stood up and said that the Ministry had reminded him of his favourite passage from QF&P and he proceeded to read the same passage that I had read at the start of the Meeting. Perhaps we should let things develop naturally!

Just how heated this discussion can become and how ridiculous it can be is illustrated by a Meeting I went to in Lancaster. It was not a regular, scheduled part of the local Meeting programme, it was an additional Meeting that was designed to be longer than normal and which involved people who had come from other parts of the country (including me, of course).

I do not remember the timings exactly but after a while in silence, we were invited to move to a different room which had a kitchen to one side. Our Quaker host went into the kitchen and returned with a plate of baked bread. He then offered this to us and suggested that each of us took a turn to take a piece of bread and explain something about the act of doing it or sharing it that felt significant to them.

Of course, there is plenty of religious and spiritual symbolism in sharing bread, having your daily bread, breaking bread and so on. Personally, I found the sharing of bread a bonding activity which brought the Meeting closer together. The participants made quite a range of comments as to what was the significance was to them but, when we returned to the main Meeting Room, I felt that we had had a shared spiritual experience (and some well-baked bread).

Some people have reacted to this story with outrage. The bread was prepared Ministry, it should not be allowed! Those versed in mainstream Christianity may be completely confused at this point as they are used to services that are nothing but preparation, even when the priest has a chance to speak outside the set readings for the day, it will be something carefully worked on and considered. I doubt that there are many sermons that are made up on the spot (though it may seem otherwise).

Personally, I have no problem with a small act of preparation. Sometimes in Cardiff Meeting we have had activities around Christmas, including lighting candles to remember those we have lost or who we miss and writing wishes on a piece of glittery card to be hung on a Christmas tree (I did the glittering). To me, these prompt thoughts rather than stop them being inspired. I am not saying that the Spirit needs to be prompted, more that an activity can help people search for what needs to be said.

This also brings us to the difference between being a Quaker in the UK and elsewhere in the world. Other countries have a tradition of 'programmed worship' where there will be a set order for part of the service. Some other Meetings have those who lead the service too. The UK's Quaker tradition is a particular one and not in the majority on the planet.

Doubtless you would expect me to say that I think that we have a good balance. We have the opportunity for waiting in silence for the Spirit but just occasionally we have an activity too. I have also discussed more fully in another chapter the practice of reading from Quaker Faith & Practice each week if there is no Ministry forthcoming. Having an activity or baking some bread or doing something that brings a little preparation into the proceedings is not to doubt the work of the Spirit, it is to acknowledge that sometimes we need to prompt ourselves to listen more intently to what the Spirit is saying.

13. Yealand Conyers

"A Man Will Meet You At the Station"

For seven years I had a job travelling around Wales advising charities about how to work with young people. Like all jobs it had its frustrations, but I never tired of meeting new people or travelling. Being someone who had environmental principles, I travelled as much as I could by public transport. This is easier to do than most people who avoid public transport think, but there are some parts of Wales that are a challenge to find without a car. In these cases, I would tend to tell people my travel plans and wait for them to offer to meet me at the station. I did rely on other people giving me a lift in a whole range of places.

Did your mother ever tell you not to get into cars with strangers? I spent seven years completely flouting that advice. Yet in many ways I now look at it as a Quaker experience. Sometimes it was pretty obvious who I was going to meet – once a bald man with a dachshund on a lead stood at Merthyr station holding a sign that said 'HEALD' – and other times I had to rely on someone coming up to me and saying 'you must be the person I am here to meet'. Twice I asked someone why they assumed that I was me and they simply replied that I looked like the person who e-mailed them.

Yes, I know what you are thinking, I could have just sent them a photo or a description of who I was, but there never seemed to be time to organise that. However, I did once mention it in Ministry. I was taking a train journey to Ammanford the next day and all I knew was that a woman named Amanda would meet me at the station and drive me to the theatre project where she worked. One of my reasons for visiting was that I was assessing them for a grant.

On the Sunday before the visit, there was Ministry about God and nature and how much easier it is to feel closer to God in a beautiful place. This has always rankled with me a little since I think that it is all too easy to ignore God's most beautiful creation and also the hardest to love part of that creation – human-beings. Wonder at the beauty of nature, but never forget that we are part of it. I am of the opinion that not only is there that of God in everyone but that most people are basically decent. As most newspapers work hard to tell you that you are constantly under threat and in danger from other human beings (it sells more newspapers if you are frightened), this is quite a radical view.

However, I told the Meeting that the next day I would be met in a remote town by a woman who I did not know and that she was going to take me to a place that I had never been to before. Yes, she could be intending to kidnap and murder me, but I would rather believe that she would not do so. I said that if she did kidnap and murder me then I would return at the next Meeting and tell people. Not everyone listens carefully to Ministry.

On the Monday, I took the train to Ammanford. It was a very pleasant experience given that after Swansea I had the train all to myself and the Guard promised to come and tell me when we reached Ammanford, so I could concentrate on watching the scenery. I was the only one leaving the train there, there was only one person on the platform waiting for me. Of course, she did not kidnap me and murder me and I knew that she would not do so –

no-one murders someone before they have been given their grant.

This rather long introduction comes about because when I visited Yealand Conyers, I was told that a man would meet me at the nearest station and no more than that. On this occasion, I was not alone, I had met a fellow Quaker at a Quaker Renewal UK gathering in Lancaster and she had been in contact with the Yealand Conyers Meeting to arrange some overnight accommodation at the Meeting House. A man would meet us at the nearest station. How do you spot a Quaker leaving a train? Someone had once told me that they knew who I was as soon as I had entered their university building in a bright blue anorak singing 'Here comes the hotstepper', but what is 'typical' Quaker behaviour?

We were met and driven across nature reserves to Yealand Conyers. Having never lived in or around Lancashire or Cumbria, it is not a part of the world that I know very well and I was immediately struck by the beauty of the place. The Meeting House itself was in a small village and the building next to it clearly doubled as accommodation, a school and a focus for the local community. I was shown to my accommodation, which would be a camp bed and a sleeping bag in an old part of the school. Sometimes this kind of generosity is all you need for a good night's sleep.

The next morning, I had a chance to look at the Meeting House itself. It was from the seventeenth century and claimed to be a place where George Fox had once sheltered from an angry mob (I have found a few with that claim). It was surrounded by a graveyard with those simple, semi-circular gravestones that I rather like as a statement of both equality and simplicity. Most interestingly for me, the Meeting House was open some time before the Meeting started, so my Friend took the opportunity to go in an hour before the start time and make it a long Meeting. Yes I know that those well-versed in Quaker ways will tell me that technically the Meeting started the moment that she sat down early, but bear with me.

I did explore my accommodation a little. I found an old, out of tune piano and played a song on it that I had recently written – 'Unicycle Woman'. I logged on to a Quaker internet discussion group where people were having highly-exercised arguments about the peace testimony. I spent some time in and around the village before I arrived at the Meeting House for the more usual start time.

I think that Quakers should be a little careful about becoming too enamoured of their historical buildings or those who have used them. There is a danger that we become in awe of the oldest Meeting Houses and treat them as relics, rather like some would say that Anglicans or Roman Catholics do with their cathedrals. A Meeting House was, after all, a house where Quakers could meet. The Spirit is everywhere as well as in every one.

This brings us to the slightly vexed question of 'bringing greetings'. It is traditional to bring greetings from your 'home' Meeting to a Meeting that you are visiting and for them to ask you to take their greetings back to your 'home' Meeting. In my experience this does tend to lead to people standing up in Meetings and saying 'I am sure that my Meeting would send greetings if I had remembered to ask them' until after a few times doing this they just assume that their Meeting would want them to pass on greetings. I have sometimes wondered if we should have some kind of physical greeting to give – a card, for instance – but then from a sustainability point of view that is probably not very good.

My Friend had asked me if I would give greetings from Cardiff Meeting and I had forgotten to do so. This was partly because I had been thinking of the other problem – how to get from the Meeting House to the station after the service. This was a Sunday (of course) so there was also no guarantee of a train to Lancaster from where we could find a train heading homeward. My Friend had the obvious solution, as part of her introduction at the end, she asked if anyone could give us a lift to the train station.

As it happens, we were offered a lift not just to the nearest station but all the way to Lancaster. I imagine that you would probably think that Quakers are not the kind of people to kidnap and murder other Quakers. At least, they would probably be aware of the truth testimony and have to say 'Yes, I am planning to drive to Lancaster, but I will have to kidnap and murder you on the way'.

Actually, my point is rather similar to the one in the chapter about Quakers on the internet. I trust the Quaker who gave me a lift to Lancaster as much as I trust the woman who picked me up at Ammanford station. People are basically decent and – with a certain level of precaution in your life – can be trusted more than most people believe.

Human beings are part of God's beautiful creation too.

14. One Quaker and Truth

We were talking about how to write up the details of the trip to Quakers Yard for the Area Meeting Magazine (for the trip itself, see 'One Quaker and Pilgrimage'). Truthfully (watch for how casually that word is used), there had been a disappointingly low level of interest in the trip before it happened. What should we say? 'A group of Quakers', 'A few Quakers' or 'A number of Quakers' went to Quakers Yard? Was giving the impression of a larger group than the one that took part going to cause a problem?

Mulling over these issues, I asked if we were supposed to be telling the truth or whether we were trying to avoid misleading others. The response from a fellow Quaker was that we should avoid being misleading. It was true that 'a number of Quakers travelled' but it was designed to be vague enough to mislead others into thinking more were involved than was actually the case. Welcome to the complicated world of the truth testimony!

I remember first hearing about this distinction in the mid-1990s, long before I became a Quaker. Bill Clinton was President of the USA and he was having trouble with accounting for statements that he had made about his interaction with the intern Monica Lewinsky. He had been truthful in that his words had been true, but they had also been misleading. Someone pointed out to me that Christians believed in 'not bearing false witness' (not lying) but that other religions asked that you 'not seek to mislead'.

When we talk about being committed to the truth, it initially seems quite simple. Who ate the last cookie? That would be me. This does allow some leeway. I was once told that Roman Catholic scholars asked what the commitment to truth should be if you were shielding Jewish refugees during the Second World War when the Nazis arrived at your door and asked if you had seen any Jews in the neighbourhood. Actually, I think that that one is simple as well (though extreme) – what is lying about replying, 'I am not going to tell you'. I imagine that it would get you into trouble, but I do not see why that should be a situation in which you would be forced to lie (not least because the Nazis are probably going to come in and break up your home anyway if they suspect enough to be asking you). However, truth tends not to be challenged in such circumstances. Have you ever tried to buy a second hand car?

I am not saying that second hand car salespeople[26] are Nazis, but I am saying that the interaction that you have when you buy a second hand car presumes from the beginning that you are both lying. Indeed, if you do not lie then you can confuse the whole sale.

I observed this the last time that I bought a second hand car. I knew how much I wanted to pay and I also knew the kind of car that I wanted. However, the salesman (see footnote) decided when he saw me the kind of car that I wanted and also how much he wanted me to pay. He showed me a number of cars and tried to persuade me of the quality of each of them. I was careful not to show too much enthusiasm, lest it encourage him to up the price (that you are even expected to mislead people with your sounds).

---

[26] I am yet to meet a female second hand car salesperson, but let us be strictly gender neutral in the hope that they do exist.

Note that he asked me, 'How much were you expecting to pay?' If I had replied 'Five thousand pounds' or 'three thousand pounds' he would probably have shown me the same car. All the car-buying magazines advise you not to give away your price and so I gave a non-committal answer around the type of car I would like. Is that misleading with your words or just negotiation?

Eventually we agreed on the car that I wanted to buy. At this point he started to find a long list of 'extras' that I would need and this added an extra 20% to the price. Here is where being a Quaker helped. I said – not untruthfully – 'that's not a price I am prepared to pay'. He clearly saw this as a negotiating tactic rather than a statement of fact and took out some of the extras. Then he changed a few other details before finally making a big show of 'going to see his manager' to ask for permission for an extra discount. I watched where he went and it was to a break room, where I presume he sat down and had a cup of tea for five minutes in the hope that the delay would seem impressive.

Finally, I did buy a car and I am sure that he gained a good commission from the sale, but that is not the point (for me, at least). It was only a sale reached through the presumption that both parties would hide their true intentions. If Quaker chocolate manufacturers were once prized for their honest dealings, then this was the opposite.

You are probably asking what happens if one side of the transaction is honest. I once tried that with a double glazing salesman. I told him from the start that I was not going to buy any windows from him but that I was interested in knowing the cost if I wanted to do so at any point in the future. He took this as a bargaining move rather than the truth. After a long discussion of how to replace my current windows, he quoted me a price of

£5,200. I explained that I was not looking to buy, but I was interested in the price. He suggested £4,500. Again, I repeated that perhaps in the future I might replace my windows, but not now. More bargaining clearly as he dropped the price to £4,200.

This continued. Every time I said that I was not looking to buy, he dropped the price a bit more because he clearly thought that I was lying to try to get a better deal out of him. He gave up at £3,000, which was also a curious thought for me – why would I buy from a company that would initially try to overcharge me by £2,200? He said to me, "You really aren't going to buy any windows, are you?" I avoided the temptation to reply, "That's what I've been saying to you."

In fact, I think that the Quaker testimony of truth becomes more fascinating the more you look at it in terms of the day-to-day lies we are expected to tell. Often we are encouraged to 'bend the truth' to 'spare other people's feelings' or to gain an easier, smoother life. Sometimes it is to spare our own feelings - how many people respond to a beggar's question 'can you spare a bit of change?' with 'Yes, but I don't want to' rather than 'No, sorry'.

Can we split the choice to avoid the guilt of avoiding giving money to the beggar from the choice to say 'I love those socks!' when given an unwanted Christmas present? Is there a difference between sparing our own feelings and trying not to insult the feelings of others? After all, we probably all know someone who boasts 'I say what I think, me!' and who therefore has few friends and is generally disliked as being an arrogant bore.

I am not sure that we can make a distinction, but I do think that we can be careful. As with the extreme example earlier about Nazis, you can find wording that is truthful and yet thoughtful. More to the point, it is always worth trying to look at what lies behind the testimony. In this case, I think that the avoidance of deceit and keeping to an honourable truth is where we should be heading. Does that mean answering the question 'does my bum look big in this?' with 'yes and the top's doing nothing for your face either' or does it mean advising someone to try another garment? We can surely aim for words that are truthful and not misleading, but also not cruel.

As with so much, what seems like an easy proposition - we do not lie - becomes something more challenging the more you look at it. I recommend a little game for the next week of your life - try to identify all the times that you bend the truth or make excuses, whether it be for your betterment ('oh traffic was terrible this morning' rather than 'I couldn't be bothered to get out of bed this morning') or to avoid hurting others ('I'd love to come to your party but I've already agreed to another event' instead of 'you make boring conversation and your jelly is horrible so no, I would not like to pop over on Saturday night'). I suspect that if you are honest (and remember it covers misleading people too so no exaggeration for the comfort of your ego), you will find it harder than you imagine.

No-one said that being a Quaker would be easy ... which I like because religion should be challenging to how we behave rather than just an affirmation of what we are doing already.

Honest.

15. Brixton & Streatham

"Friends Will Be Friends"

There are a few versions of the story told as to why we are called 'Friends'. The capitalisation also becomes a little unwieldy when also talking about friends and, of course, social media has made it all the more complicated by insisting that we are 'friends' with people who we have never even met. I had always thought that we were Friends In the Truth or Friends Of the Truth and, indeed, we were said to be like the first century Christians who seemed like such friends that they could not be separated.

If I ever start a notice, an announcement or Ministry, I always start with 'Friends'. It seems an appropriate way to talk to my fellow Friends and, of course, I sign my e-mails with 'In Friendship' (not 'In F/friendship' as some do because I do not want to distinguish my Friends from my friends. Not all my friends are Friends, but all Friends are friends. Is it becoming confusing yet?).

I visited Streatham & Brixton Meeting early on in my travels as a Quaker. I had only been to three or four Meetings at the most prior to this, but I was staying in London for the weekend and I had decided to track down my nearest Meeting on the Sunday morning. My reason for being in London was a concert by the Super Furry Animals at the Brixton Academy and so, naturally, I had booked a B&B in Brixton.

I have to say that the B&B was a tribute to simplicity. Gone were extraordinary concepts such as ensuite facilities or indeed any facilities that might make the stay anything easier than lying on a bed high above a busy road. Now I enjoy going to a toilet two floors away from my room in the middle of the night as much as the next man, but this felt like simplicity going too far. However, I decided that on the Sunday morning I would try to find the Quaker Meeting in Brixton.

I should probably also tell you the political background. This was the Sunday after the 2015 General Election. For those who do not remember this, have blocked it out or who are reading this many years in the future having bought it from a fundraising stand at a Quaker charity fayre, the 2015 General Election was a disappointment for many. There had been five years of a coalition government between Conservatives and Liberal Democrats and many people expected this coalition to be swept away by an incoming Labour government. It did not work out that way or as Canon Giles Fraser summarised it, he went to the polling booths thinking that no-one could vote without thinking about the million people who lived in poverty and woke up the next morning realising just how many of his fellow citizens did not care that there were a million people living in poverty. The Conservative Party won an overall majority.

I had booked my trip to the see the Super Furry Animals long before David Cameron had called his election and so I had set off the day after election night feeling both deflated (by the result) and tired (having stayed up to watch the result). I decided to be both philosophical and to find the local Quaker Meeting on the Sunday.

I nearly did not find it and I nearly gave up hope. Walking down what seemed like an endless suburban road from the Tube station with my case dragging behind me, I started to wonder why I was doing this, whether I would ever find a Quaker Meeting in a haystack of housing and also whether anyone there would want a stranger walking in off the street and sitting in their favourite chair.

In fact, with eleven o'clock approaching, I had decided to give up. I had no idea where I was other than on a long road from the Tube station which should have taken me past a Quaker Meeting House. I am not sure if I had any ideas in my early days about what a Meeting House should look like (I now resolve on the conclusion that there is no typical Meeting House) but I could not see one and went to look at a bus stop to see if there was any indication of when I might catch a bus back into the city.

When I reached the bus stop, I turned around to get my bearings and there was a sign, amid a modern development of housing and flats, that said 'Quaker Meeting House' and had a big arrow pointing away from the road. Clearly they had had difficulty with people becoming lost when looking for them before.

I followed the sign and entered the building nervously. So much about our experience of Quaker Meetings depends on that first welcome and I hope that people who volunteer to take on that role each week are aware of how important they are. On this occasion, there was an outstretched hand and a greeting of 'Welcome, Friend'.

It would be hard for me to overstate how much it means to a travelling Quaker to be welcomed as a 'Friend'. Before I discovered Quakers (or they discovered me), I had visited many churches and I have strong memories of walking into them and seeing a small group of worshippers turn to look at me and wonder who I am. Not all churches are like that of course, but the feeling of inclusion that so many Meeting Houses manage is something special. I suspect that when faith wavers, the support and community of the Meeting keeps a lot of people engaged.

That said, I went into the Meeting Room and immediately sat on the chair reserved for the doorkeeper. I was asked to move. However, at the end of the worship, there were big apologies for having to ask me to move, which was not quite the same as sitting in someone else's chair.

I mentioned that this was the weekend after the General Election of 2015 and that if you were not a supporter of the Conservative government, then it was a time of great disappointment. Indeed, at the Super Furry Animals gig the night before, the lead singer Gruff Rhys had told the audience how shocked he was by the result. The concert was being broadcast live on Belgian television so he apologised to the Belgians for the actions of the UK and asked the crowd to boo David Cameron. There is a claim to fame for you, I have booed a serving British Prime Minister live on Belgian television.

One of those attending the Meeting on that Sunday morning had been at a demonstration in central London the day before. There had been, seemingly inevitably but also sadly, a violent element who had turned up and caused trouble, leading to lurid Daily Mail headlines about the thugs and hooligans who opposed democracy. The Quaker pondered on the unlikeliness of Quakers forming a 'violent mob' but sadly to the tabloid newspapers there is no nuance.

However, you can also not overstate the comfort of finding like-minded people. I am sure that within that group there were a variety of views and had we had a political discussion then we would have found a very wide range of thoughts on all sorts of topics but for me, alone and lost on a Sunday in London, this felt like I was being told that it was okay to feel lost, alone and upset by events in the world.

Truly I was among Friends.

16. Quakers and Creativity

At the first Quaker Meeting I went to, God gave me the ending for my first book. It was one of the reasons why I went back to my Quaker Meeting a second time. Let me explain ...

I first went to a Quaker Meeting in 2012. I was not sure what to find but I saw the silence as my chance to try to sort out some of my feelings about religion, faith and God (note : always 'God', never 'he' because God is not male or female and also never 'Lord' because God does not have a place in the English aristocracy). I had written a book two years previously after the double distress of losing my job and my father being moved into a care home. I needed something to do to cope and so I wrote. However, the book remained unpublished and having thought that I was guided to write, I sat in Meeting silently despairing of my seemingly stalled mission.

It was in this despair that God gave me a new ending for my book. I had based one of the main characters on a friend who had moved to Cardiff from Devon and through this character I wanted to portray the way that a vibrant city like Cardiff pulled in people from all over the rest of the country. I noted - contemptuous of my own failure - that the book did not even make sense now as that friend had moved back to Devon. That is your ending was God's reply and it was. It is hard to explain to you without going into detail about the rest of the book, but that was a perfect and brilliant ending to it. No wonder I went back to the Quaker Meeting the next week!

Quakers seem to have an odd relationship with creativity. Although not puritans (and you can make people very cross online if you call Quakers puritans), some of an occasional historical dislike of music, dancing and art seems to have come through to us in the modern age. Quakers wrote a lot but I still find talking about God inspiring me creatively to be one of those things that makes some fellow Quakers raise their eyebrows.

Many years ago there was an American television programme entitled 'Joan of Arcadia'. It revolved around a simple idea – every week Joan would meet God and God would ask her to perform a simple task. This task rarely made sense to Joan but by the end of the episode, the viewer usually realised how it fitted into a bigger plan. God was not the all light and majesty kind of God but would appear to Joan through ordinary people. One week God would be a young man, the next an old lady, the week after a small child ... if you wanted 'that of God in everyone' illustrated, it was a pretty perfect demonstration, though I do not think that the programme-makers were making a deliberate reference to Quakers.

Early on in the first season, Joan asks God to prove that he is indeed a God – 'do a miracle or something' she says, rather like most humans like to occasionally challenge God to some kind of magic display which will satisfy their belief. God points at a tree and asks Joan to consider how special it is.

"It's only a tree," replies Joan.

"When did you last create one, then?" asks God.

It may sound initially rather superior if I tell you that I think that creativity is where we touch that divine gift of creation. There are other ways to do it but for me, that moment of going from nothing to something is a little bit of divinity rubbed off on us. I also write songs and I can visualise for you my songbook with the start and the end of a song in it and with the middle two verses missing. Within a few weeks, those verses are written. That move from nothing to something is pretty incredible and perhaps under rated somewhat. Is it wrong to say that sometimes the inspiration truly is God-given and we should do more than praise God for the gifts that have been given to us?

I have no doubt that God wishes me to be creative and to entertain and inform other people through my words and music. If I ever feel like Joan in her menial tasks, I consider that they make part of a bigger picture or plan that I cannot see. I also remember the week when Joan complained about being asked to build a boat with the words, "Why can you never give me something that is a big deal?" and God replies, "Last time I asked someone to build a boat it was a big deal."

It would be easy to believe that creativity is God-given if you are talking about great art or music. You know the kind of thing, it inspires and amazes you and inspires emotions in you that take you deeper into your knowledge or your appreciation of beauty. However, I want to tell you that even the most menial creativity is a gift from God. The same God who inspired the majesty, power and beauty of Durham Cathedral also inspired a comedy song about courgettes.

In 2016, I decided to write a song called 'The Girl Who Brings the Courgettes to the Party'. I had held a party and a friend had brought along a bag of courgettes with her. At this point some people would ask 'why' when I would rather say that you should not doubt the sincerity of women with bags of courgettes. As she left the party, she said, 'you should write a song called 'Courgette Girl".

I tend to avoid writing songs that people have suggested. I prefer to see something and then work out how it could be funny so I ignored this suggestion for a long time. Then, as I was walking between two parts of my workplace, I decided to pass the time by trying to write a song about courgettes. I had a bass beat, I had a rhythm guitar and then I had lyrics about 'the girl who brings the courgettes to the party'.

However, my lyrics had two particular problems coming from the following verse –

What's in the bag then, Courgette Girl?

Can we even start to guess?

If you're a gambling man, place your bets

We pay out evens on courgettes.

The problem with this was that I disliked the sexism of 'gambling man' and also the reference to gambling (being a Quaker). There were other things wrong with the song, but let me just use this minor one to show you the level that God works on with creativity.

I was at a Quaker Peace & Social Witness conference in York while I was thinking about this song. This was a different one to the QPSW conference mentioned in the 'Invisibility' chapter but it was the same principle. At the end of the conference we had a silence, Ministry and a chance to hold hands in a circle to show how we are joined together as a Quaker circle.

I had not really thought about 'the courgette gambling problem' until that moment when we came to hold hands. As soon as my hand touched someone else's I heard –

If you like gambling, place your bets

We pay out evens on courgettes.

The joke is the same as it was, namely that you have a pretty safe bet that someone named 'Courgette Girl' is going to have courgettes in her bag. However, now the sexism is removed and also it invites people who like gambling to do so rather than promoting gambling. These are tiny amendments (and they did come with others), but I knew at that moment that the song was as good as it should be.

The God of Courgettes? Why not? Why do we assume that the inspiration to build the great cathedrals of the world is God-given but that the impulse to tell a joke that makes people happy is not divine? 'The Girl Who Brings the Courgettes To The Party' has entertained plenty of people and is hopefully something that has made people happy. Is it too much to say that there is something divine behind this creativity? I am not boasting that anything I do is better than anyone else could do, but I do wonder if maybe we should credit creative people with divine inspiration a bit more often. We are sometimes halfway there – Muses are perhaps a way of capturing the divine in a mystical form, but why not?

Quakers once had this reputation for being austere and plain, perhaps because of the tradition of plain speaking and plain living. Personally, I think that we have been granted a wide range of talents and that God calls us to use them as best we can. Perhaps we should be more vocal about their divine source, but for me God is in songs about courgettes too.

17. Eastbourne

"Quaker Dogs"

The friend who I was staying with in Eastbourne was not going to come to the Quaker Meeting in Eastbourne, but he was still curious as to what happened there. I have dragged friends to Meeting before – one of my friends has been to four different Meetings in two different countries and is nowhere nearer being a Quaker! However, I am never insistent and I always understand that it is not most people's cup of tea. All the same, my friend was surprised to know that there was a Meeting in Eastbourne. I have learned over the years that predicting where there are Meetings is quite hard. What, he wanted to know, would be the order of service?

To me, one of the delights of travelling around the country visiting different Quaker Meetings is that there are some things that are always the same and some things that are always different in each location. I told my friend about my early attempts to describe Quakers while travelling with friends to the South Belfast Meeting. One thing I had been insistent on was that Quakers were in the Christian tradition. The first Quaker we met at South Belfast announced, "I'm a Buddhist Quaker".

Eastbourne was no exception to this rule of exceptions. However, first I tried to explain to my friend what I thought might happen at the Meeting. I also speculated as to when Quakers had arrived in Eastbourne and where they worshipped. I think that all my speculation was as wrong as when I told other friends that we would meet Christians in Belfast. I would be wiser than to say that now, though not wise enough just to avoid all predictions about Quakers.

The Quaker Meeting House in Eastbourne was central, but hidden away rather in a back alley. Some of the development around that area was modern, but it was a narrow lane and I was not surprised when I found out later that a lot of people knew it for a garage that was based down there at one time. You could imagine mechanics with hoods up on cars, letting their tools spill out into the road.

However, there was no mistaking the brick wall that had a doorway with 'Friends Meeting House' written across it. I thought that it might be a 1930s brick built construction, but then I also thought that it might be a 1980s brick built construction. From the outside it was rather anonymous – well, anonymous but for the name and the open door.

Inside, the building was very different. The long front went back to no more than a corridor that joined two wings going at right angles. A square was completed on the other side with an open courtyard in the middle. In the two wings were the two essentials for a Quaker building – the Meeting Room and the kitchen.

However, the real surprise was to come when someone mentioned the dog.

It is very hard to talk to some people about animals and religion. There is no doubt that animals (especially people's pets) give a huge amount of love and it is hard not to see that as part of a divine plan. However, if you suggest that animals have no soul or that there is not 'that of God' in them[27], then you can receive a furious

---

[27] See 'What is a Quaker?' for more on 'that of God in everyone'.

rebuke from some people. We are the creatures with free will, but when you have had someone angrily reply, "Are you saying my dog is evil?" then you know that rational discussion on this point may be hard.

I was once cornered by another Quaker about my belief in pacifism. Why, she wanted to know, did we not execute terrorists as we would put down a sick dog. When I replied that I believed in 'that of God in everyone' but that this gave a special status to human-beings and not animals, she responded angrily about how dogs had souls and also went to heaven. I decided that it was best not to ask her about her beef sandwich and whether cows had souls as well. Talking about animals and religion is complicated.

One of my favourite comments on animals and religion came in a sermon that I heard in church as a child. Though I do not believe that it is true, I think that it is a lovely thought. The vicar who was preaching the sermon said that he had decided long ago that there was a separate heaven for animals and that it was presided over by St Francis.

This is all connected to Eastbourne because Eastbourne has a Quaker dog. Apparently, the dog is quite famous and has even become a Member of the Religious Society of Friends. It seemed to be very much an animal-friendly meeting as there were actually two dogs there that morning.

To have two dogs sitting in a circle might seem like a recipe for disaster and certainly there were some suspicious looks between the dogs at the start of the Meeting. However, either they were used to sitting in silence for an hour or the peace of God that passes all understanding had really passed in to them and they settled down while the Meeting went on. They even stayed quiet when Ministry was given – something I have seen small children struggle with, so it was even more impressive.

At the end of the Meeting, the Meeting rose and shook hands. However, someone had told me to hold my hand out because, sure enough, the larger of the two dogs went around and placed his paw in every outstretched hand (he must be the dog that is the Quaker Member, the other one must have been an Attender – apologies to non-Quaker readers, that is a bit of an insider joke).

I had many thoughts about this. As a recent convert to a mix of vegetarian/veganism, I did wonder that we show such love to dogs and even invite them into our religious worship, but can be so cruel to the animals that we eat. I am not sure that it is a religious point, but the older that I get, the more that I find that disparity troubling (I do like the Quaker conferences that offer two dietary options – vegetarian food or vegan food – but I have met as many Quaker carnivores as anything else). However, I did also wonder about the ethics of bringing a dog to worship.

Consider for a moment that a 'gathered' Meeting is supposed to be an act of worship together as much as a church service would be, how can a dog be part of it? Then again, I was told that in the original Quaker Meetings, there would have been farmers who would have thought nothing of taking their dogs with them.

Perhaps letting a dog be a Member of the Religious Society of Friends brought up more questions, but why not have a well-behaved dog in a meeting? Why not acknowledge the love that pets can give us? After all, would we turn away a guide dog or a hearing dog if it came to a Meeting with a Quaker? I could see that people might object if everyone wanted to bring their dog or if a member of the Meeting was afraid of dogs or had an allergy, but I did not find the principle a troubling one.

Having decided that I was okay with meeting a Quaker dog, I headed back to meet my friend for lunch. A few days later I told a fellow Quaker about meeting a Quaker dog, thinking that she would also approve and find it kind of cute and sentimental. I had forgotten that you should never mix pets and religion. She was horrified! What if the dog attacked someone? What if someone was frightened of dogs? Dogs have no soul, how can they properly partake? Is there that of God in them?

Sometimes I think that there may be that of God in all of us, but we could also sometimes do with that of dogs in us too.

18. One Quaker and Pilgrimage – Quakers Yard

How many places in the UK are named after churches? I would be sure that if I asked you to stop for a moment and think of some place names, you would find a few that have churches in their title - Whitchurch, Newchurch, Oldchurch, Christchurch ... and that is just to start.

People make fun of the village of 'Eglwyswrw' in west Wales for having only one vowel in its name (in English), but that is just the church of St Wrw. Allow saints into the equation and there are plenty of St Mary, Trinity and St Peters out there. Christianity has shaped our landscape and it has been a church-based Christianity too. Here then is my challenge to you – can you think of anywhere that has a name based on its Quaker connections?

I had been through the town of Quakers Yard (or Quakers' Yard depending on which sign you believe) on the way between Cardiff and Merthyr Tydfil by train and also as part of the long distance walking route The Taff Trail. This was long before I was a Quaker and I am not sure that I even gave second thought to what the name meant. A friend of mine lived in Quakers Yard and I cannot remember ever asking her where the unusual name came from. However, I can now say that this is the only place I have been to which is named after Quakers. We have a long way to go to overtake all the Whitchurches in the UK, but one is a start.

Do Quakers do pilgrimage? I am not sure why, but it seems as though Christian pilgrimage has become more popular in recent years. Perhaps this is just me knowing people in their mid-life who are looking to do something major and dramatic, perhaps this is just me being more aware of it since I visited Santiago De Compostela (not on a pilgrimage - ever the rebel), but I feel as though pilgrimage is more visible than it was twenty or thirty years ago.

Modern day pilgrims are not always religious though. I think that most note with a wry smile the sign in St Davids Cathedral which explains that two pilgrimages to St Davids are the same as one to Rome and that two pilgrimages to Rome are the same as one to Jerusalem. Quakers would probably also find those kind of calculations odd as we do not seem to be the kind of people who worship 'places' – certainly our Meeting Houses speak of simplicity in the way that some of the great cathedrals speak of wealth and power. Have I ever heard a fellow Quaker announce that they were going on a pilgrimage?

We have no 'holy land' (and I am sure that some, like me, would object to the whole idea that some land is 'holy', all land is holy). The oldest Meeting Houses do evoke a sense of history and I have been to several places where George Fox is said to have been arrested, but I would not describe it as a pilgrimage. Perhaps that is just an unsentimental view of our history. Swarthmoor Hall runs tours of the places that were significant in George Fox's work in Lancashire and Cumbria and refer to them as '1652 Pilgrimages'. A friend asked me if this was because each day finished just before five o'clock, but the history is clearly deeper than that. I suppose that I do find the places where the early Quakers went, met and studied are interesting[28] but they are only of historical interest to me

[28] I do know of someone who has told me that the foundation of the Religious Society of Friends and, indeed, the first use of that title came from William Erbury of Cardiff and not George Fox. As will be mentioned in passing during

and not spiritual interest. Does that make it a historical tour rather than a pilgrimage?

My reason for being in Santiago De Compostela was for a holiday and not for pilgrimage. I was travelling around Galicia (north-west Spain) with a friend and Santiago is a convenient stopping point, as well as being a beautiful town in its own right. Did I want to queue up and see the remains of St James? No. When I remarked to my friend that it was probably not St James's remains anyway, he replied, 'ah, but it is the unlikeliness of it that tests your faith'. Can you imagine if we kept George Fox's hat and required all Quakers to visit it once in their lifetime?

This brings me back to Quakers Yard. It is a small town in the south Wales valleys, a little south of Merthyr Tydfil. It is also the only place I know that is named after Quakers. There is some fascinating Quaker history in the area and I set off one Saturday with a group from Cardiff Meeting to take a small tour around the area.

In the best tradition of the railway system, the station named 'Quakers Yard' (no apostrophe) is not very close to the town of Quakers' Yard (apostrophe). The walk between is along an old tramline and takes you under one of Brunel's mighty viaducts taking the main railway line across the river Taff and above your walking route. It is a quiet spot where you can hear the sound of the river and the far off sounds of people, without necessarily meeting any people coming the other way. At the time that the railway line was built, Quakers Yard was the nearest settlement and hence the name.

It would seem that a range of dissenters had started meeting in a farmhouse near to modern day Quakers Yard and that there used to be a significant population of

---

the chapter on Aberystwyth, Fox's role in Quaker history is sometimes disputed.

Quakers among them. Certainly there were enough of them to be left a piece of land in the centre of the town as a burial ground. The industrial revolution then came along and changed the area significantly - Edwardsville and Treharris were founded around the railway station and coal mining became the dominant form of employment. Still, the burial ground stood in the midst of it.

The industrial revolution was not the end of the Quaker involvement there, however. The mine owner William Harris (after whom Treharris was named - you see, after a while we stopped naming places after churches and started naming them after wealthy men) was a Quaker and the town for his workers included a number of references to Quaker history - you can still visit Fox Street, Penn Street and Fell Street.

On the day of our visit, the burial ground was how I had seen it before - maintained by someone, but also covered in litter. We had brought black bags and started to clear the area of lager cans and empty bottles of Lambrini[29]. It is an odd little spot. Once it would have been a quiet retreat perhaps but now the main by-pass road thunders past and you cannot have a moment of stillness without putting in the effort to block out the noise. We had some discussion as to whether the by-pass road had been built over part of the burial ground. It looks as though it has been, although old drawings of the area suggest that the ground may have always been a slightly odd shape.

I wondered aloud if maybe there was something symbolic about the Quakers retaining this little piece of quiet in the midst of all the traffic noise and the small town centre. 350 years of change had gone on around them but they

---

[29] For those familiar with the 'Lambrini Girls just wanna have fun' advertising, I offer the alternative slogan 'Lambrini Girls just wanna desecrate scared burial grounds'.

still kept to the silence amid the noise. You can read that as being inflexible or as being true to your principles.

There is a pub opposite the burial ground - The Quakers Yard Inn (no apostrophe). On this occasion, the group of us did not go in as we were looking for the woodland walk up to Treharris (and in true valleys tradition, the walk is upwards) but I had heard from other Quakers that they are always very friendly towards 'real' Quakers and that their range of activities includes 'Quaker Karaoke'. A Friend pointed out to me that 'Quaker karaoke' is a kind of model for how Quaker worship should proceed - we are handed the microphone, but the words are already there from the Spirit.

We walked up to Treharris by the woodland route. You can walk there along the road, but this does bring you to a rather sad sign which has not been updated for a while. I know that it needs an update because it ends with an explanation of how the coal mine in Treharris is the most technologically-advanced in the world and is set to continue to produce coal and make money for some time to come. I am not sure when this information board was put in place but the coal mine was shut in the early 1990s and there is now no sign of the large-scale profits that were boasted (and, to be fair, were being made right up to the point of closure).

Fox Street, Penn Street and Fell Street are a network of three streets on a grid pattern in Treharris. They are standard valleys terraced houses and you do walk along them wondering if the residents know that they are named after Quakers. Mind you, all the guides note that Fell Street is not named after Margaret Fell, one of the prominent Quaker founders, but local Quaker Lydia Fell. Fox Street has a Co-Op shop, which might have a tenuous link to Quaker thoughts on alternative economic models, but it also has a pub so perhaps there is nothing there really other than three names.

The curious question is where the Quakers of Quakers Yard are now. There is no Meeting House and no trace other than in the name and the presence of the burial ground that Quakers were once there. I have searched online for some history of the Quakers of the area but other than the note that the burial ground ceased to be a meeting place for Quakers after 1891, there is no sign of what happened to them. Perhaps the Meeting just dwindled in numbers, perhaps the disused chapels of Treharris tell a story of religious decline that affected everyone, perhaps the Quakers moved elsewhere ... it is hard to know. There is only one Meeting in the Valleys now and that is some distance away in Trealaw and only monthly.

We cleared up the burial ground, had our tour around the neighbourhood and then headed home. Was that a pilgrimage? If so, what did we learn along the journey and how did we come away from it changed? Is this not what pilgrimage is really about? Yes, if you reach Santiago De Compostela, have your pilgrimage passport stamped and queue up to see the remains of St James (unlikely to be him), then you have achieved something and something that probably equates to a number of pilgrimages to Rome and more chance of getting to heaven, but ... what does it matter? Pilgrimage is surely about the journey and how you change along the way. If it were just about visiting then everyone would take the train to Santiago as I did.

In that sense, I think that a Quaker view of pilgrimage might be that once again mainstream religion is making a priority of the symbols over the experience. For a Quaker, surely the pilgrimage journey is life itself.

In conclusion, I do not believe in pilgrimage. I am also going to book myself a '1652 Pilgrimage'. Life is contradictory.

19 Aberystwyth

"The Quakers not on Quaker Street"

If Cardiff Meeting is home, then Aberystwyth Meeting is Home from Home. Rather, it is the Meeting that I have been to the second most times. I have been there with different people too – with a friend who I was staying with in Aber, on my own and with a girlfriend on the way to the Machynlleth Comedy Festival. Aberystwyth is a Meeting that I return to frequently, it seems.

When I visit a Meeting House, I always like to ask people if they know its history. Usually I end up asking someone who only started attending three weeks previously and has no clue, but sometimes I end up with a fascinating story. I do not know the story of Aberystwyth's Meeting House but I would take a few guesses.

In Aberystwyth town centre, there is a street called 'Stryd y Crynwyr' which, in English, means 'Quaker Street'. This is not where the Meeting House is nor is there any sign of any Quaker influence there, but if I were a gambler (and therefore probably not a Quaker), I would bet that that was once a Meeting House site. It is not as obvious as finding a street called 'Meeting House Lane' (found two of those on my travels), but I would make that guess.

Certainly west Wales is on the edge of an area of great Quaker activity. It is not too far north to Dolgellau, which was once home to a very active Quaker community, most of whom emigrated to America and founded the University of Bryn Mawr among other institutions. I seem to recall that 'Bryn Mawr' was the name of the farm owned by the organiser of the emigration, but there is an answer for you if anyone ever demands that you name a university named after a farm. Until fairly recently, the tourist office in Dolgellau had a permanent exhibition about the Quaker history of the area but sadly this was removed and not replaced when the information centre was closed.

While we are on the subject of American universities with Welsh connections, Yale is named after Wrexham resident Elihu Yale, who was a benefactor. Sadly in Wrexham itself, the only thing named after him is a pub. You would have thought that when the local college was relaunched as a university in the 2000s, they would have at least had a try at naming themselves Yale. The publicity from the legal case would have at least put them on the map.

However, I do not know the history of Quakers in Aberystwyth beyond the street that is named after them. Nowadays, the Meeting House in Aberystwyth is in the suburb of Penparcau. Penparcau lies on the edge of the main town area and I would guess that it was a 1960s or 1970s development of additional housing as Aberystwyth expanded. Since then, of course, the town has expanded even further but set on a hillside in Penparcau is a Meeting House that looks a little like a post-war Parish Centre from the side. From the front, it is a touch grander. The hillside is important because you look up at it from the street, which is a slightly odd sensation. Many old churches near the coast are built in dips so that the Vikings could not see them from out at sea (the best example of this is St David's Cathedral – I have been out in a boat from that coast and the whole cathedral is genuinely 'buried' out of sight from boats sailing by). Building a Meeting House near the coast on a hillside makes it sound like a beacon to all those around. If you know west Wales it also says that there is a real lack of flat land, but let us go with the romantic image instead.

On each occasion I have been to Aberystwyth Meeting, I have been welcomed at the door. Once it was so sunny that the doorway was surrounded by Quakers enjoying the sunshine before Meeting. If you have to climb up steps to reach a doorway, a handshake is welcome (though I have a vague memory that once I managed to park on the same level as the Meeting House).

I have always found that Aberystwyth Meeting reflects its local area. There are older people, there are those who have moved west for an alternative lifestyle and there are students from the university there too. It has always come across as a vibrant mix. Mind you, the first time I went there I was told that after the tea and coffee had been drunk, there was a 'threshing meeting' to decide on contentious issues that needed to be discussed. I was too new to Quakers at that time to know what a 'threshing meeting' was and I was too polite to ask what was so contentious. The fact that the Meeting seemed to be thriving on the next time I returned, suggests that all was settled amicably.

Aberystwyth also provided me with one of my favourite examples of Meetings and ministry. I had settled down and the Meeting started in silence as ever. Not long into the silence, a woman rose to talk about George Fox. I mentioned Fox back in the introduction and he can occasionally be a controversial figure among Quakers. However, this woman said how much she admired George Fox.

After she had sat down, there followed a long period of silence. There were probably no more than twenty people in the room, but you could feel their calm concentration and spiritual waiting as they contemplated her words or thought of their own. The end of the hour approached and there had been no more ministry. It was time to shake hands and end the Meeting.

Except that just before an Elder signalled that the Meeting was to end, another woman rose to speak. She said that she did not like George Fox, she thought of him as a 'ranter' (in a religion based on individual experience, a ranter is someone who puts their individual experiences above those of anyone else and does not have the Quaker disciplines of equality or checking their thoughts with their Meeting). This woman would much rather follow the example of Jesus Christ.

This prompted someone else to speak about whether it was a false comparison to compare Fox to Christ, after all, George Fox was a devout Christian and would surely have seen himself as spreading Christ's teaching rather than replacing it. Another person rose to give their view of Fox, another talked about where we should find inspiration from people ... and so on. It was soon twenty minutes since the Meeting had been due to end. There are some Quakers who refuse to use the phrase 'we meet for an hour' because sometimes we meet for as long as it takes! It was also my favourite example of how a seemingly 'quiet' Meeting needs just one piece of Ministry to become much noisier.

When the tourist centre in Dolgellau was closed, I complained about the loss of Quaker heritage. As a slightly bizarre compensation, they sent me a set of leaflets about Quakers in the area. One was the tale of how one Quaker would walk for ten or eleven miles every Sunday morning to reach Meeting. That kind of devotion does always shame me. The Meeting House in Aberystwyth is a couple of miles outside the town centre. I have always driven there. Well, as you know now, it is uphill!

20. One Quaker and Pacifism

It is hard to know where to start with pacifism. I have tried to write about it before and much of this chapter is based on a blog that I wrote in June 2016. However, I do find that there is a general misunderstanding of what pacifism is and its consequences.

For me, asking a pacifist 'what would you have done in 1939?' misses the point. Pacifism is about removing all violence as a way of solving problems, both on the international stage and in personal interactions. It is not just that we should never have got to the point that we did in 1939, it is that we are talking about a change in society that is more far-reaching than not fighting wars.

When I wrote my blog about pacifism in June 2016, we had just had the horror of the murder of Jo Cox MP by an extremist in Britain. In the USA, there had just been a mass shooting at an LGBT club in Orlando. Everywhere it seemed, division was becoming more important and conflict the main language of communication. Within a month we started to witness a rise in hate crime which two and a half years later police chiefs say has not gone away.

Making a case for the peaceful resolution of conflict has never felt more urgent and yet has also never felt more of an uphill struggle.

I am conscious though that Quakers have lived through such times before. In a biography of Margaret Fell, I found reference to a response she made to a letter from James Naylor. Naylor was despairing of the times that they lived in and whether the Quaker message could truly get through to people. Fell replied that you do not plant seeds when the weather is good, you plant them when the weather is bad in expectation of a harvest at a later date (she put it better than that, but I do not have the quote to hand, sorry).

I wonder if even as Quakers we have let our testimony drift somewhat. A couple of years after my original blog, I facilitated a Quaker discussion group about pacifism and discovered that someone had not attended because he thought 'military intervention is sometimes justified'. I was very disappointed that he had not attended because we would have welcomed those views. More than that though, it is a misreading of how wide and challenging the concept of pacifism should be.

Here is what I wrote back in 2016 ...

I have not written about the Orlando shootings as yet. In some ways I do not want to jump on a bandwagon and in some ways I am not sure that I have anything to add to what has already been written. I do think that it is relevant to me, partly because it was an attack on tolerance. Also, as journalist Owen Jones reminded people, a straight woman and her unborn child had died in the Admiral Duncan pub bombings in 1999 and those who attack 'gay venues' will kill anyone in their way. The extremist who kills indiscriminately threatens us all.

In many parts of the UK, we have a kind of tolerance to be proud of. It is by no means perfect and the rise in hate crimes during 2016 is sickening, but you can still generally go to gay clubs and pubs in Cardiff (and indeed Aberystwyth, which had the UK's first out lesbian Mayor) without fear of anyone trying to kill everyone there.

Since the Further Education college opened on Dumballs Road in Cardiff, I have noticed young people walking there hand in hand, including same sex couples. The events in Orlando are a reminder that the progress is good but it has a long way to go. I also noted that Owen Jones stormed off the Sky News coverage when they tried to say that the shooting was not an attack on LGBT people specifically. The Sky News coverage suggests a deeper homophobia at work in society. I think that we cannot divorce the violent attack on LGBT people from the society that it took place in.

However, I think that it goes even wider than that. People tend to have a misconception about pacifism, usually that it means passivity. I know a lot of very angry and very active pacifists who would disagree! Pacifism is also not just about war. That is when it gets the most publicity, but pacifism should be about the removal of all violence from society (or at least doing the most to remove as much of it as possible).

I do find it a little strange when people challenge me on it by asking what I would have done in 1914. The point would be not to get to the point of war in 1914 as a starting point. 1914 is an odd one too as it was the clash of empires, both with questionable attitudes to democracy (more adults could vote in elections in Germany in 1914 than in the UK) and both with unelected heads of state (and although the British King seemed a little more balanced than the German Kaiser, do recall that he had said that he would veto any legislation that gave Ireland any kind of devolution ... that one worked out really well, didn't it?).

Actually, 1939 is the one that people should throw at pacifists. There is no doubt which regime was the one worth fighting for in 1939 but, as I said before, the real answer would have been not to get to the point of war in 1939. The sad thing for me is that people do not connect all the violence in society and realise how it feeds off itself. Violence does not solve violence. Several years ago I was criticised on Facebook for posting the following about Libya : 'Oh good, we're going to use more violence to stop the violence. That'll work'. I would suggest that my sarcasm has been borne out by the chaos in Libya since. I invited David Cameron, Hilary Benn and Alun Cairns (my local MP) to tell me a year after the Syria vote if they felt that Syria was now more stable and less violent thanks to the violence that they supported. I wonder why they have not answered that one.

However, if we are going to avoid reaching a 1939 point again, we need to ask something about all violence in society. By this I mean the demonisation of certain groups in our society, whether they be immigrants, refugees, gay people, people with different coloured skin, 'the liberal elite', anyone who does not agree with our opinions ... 'if you are not like me, then you cannot be part of my country' has become the philosophy of some. Donald Trump seized on the shootings in Orlando as proof that Muslims had to be banned from entering the USA. The shooter was, of course, a US citizen who had been born in New York and the Trump idea would have not affected him. However, it sends a powerful message of fear and hatred about outsiders.

It is more than ideas though. It is the persistence of the idea that you could hit a child if you do not like what it is doing, the lack of seriousness that is still attached to a man hitting a woman with whom he does not agree, the idea that if you are outraged by a group of people you can walk into a nightclub and shoot them, attacks that express violence and anger towards women, the idea that we only solve things in other countries by dropping large amounts of bombs on them and then walking away. All violence is connected and all part of the same continuum of rage.

A while ago I met a woman who had been married to an abusive man and who cheerily told me about how well he had been brought up by his parents, who had been sure to physically discipline him when he misbehaved. I asked her if she had ever considered that being shown from an early age that the way you deal with things that you do not like is through violence might have led to the way that he would react to her doing something that he did not like by hitting her. She had never made that connection. Why would she? We are always told that violence is random and isolated and we never look at the wider context of it.

Recently we have seen English football fans rioting in France. Who is to blame? If you read the British papers, it is the French police and the Russian fans to blame. Whereas I am not going to defend the Russian fans, what did the British fans expect when they started throwing bricks at the French police and chanting 'Victory to ISIS!'? The French are on terrorist alert and have the tear gas and batons to control any trouble. Was the policing 'heavy-handed' or should the English people have avoided being violent in the first place? Theresa May seems to be sure that it is all the fault of the French police. Phew. However, read also the reports from peaceful fans who have talked of the angry and intimidating atmosphere created by England fans singing songs about violence and beating up other nations (and the usual clichés about the Second World War - England, time to get over it, you were on the 'winning' side thanks to the US, the Soviet Union, the Empire and a whole load of non-English people. If it were not for the US, you would all be spell-checking British English now). Once again, the papers support 'our brave fans' and we show that violence is okay because it is someone else's fault.

That would be a wonderfully powerful place to stop. There are politicians in the USA rushing to condemn the targeting of LGBT people in the Orlando attack who would happily deny gay people equality and who would fight for the 'traditional family' in America. I am sure that you see the point that I am trying to make about needing to stop all violence and not just warfare.

Unfortunately, today has also been a dark day in British politics with the murder of Jo Cox MP. When I saw the news of her murder, three predictions came to my mind -

i) There will be people who support Britain First and similar right-wing groups who will tweet their support for her murder. TICK, seen that, apparently she is a 'casualty of war' and therefore deserved it. Hmm ... women deserve the violence they receive ... eerily familiar from other kinds of violence against women?

ii) The suspect will be white and therefore will be excused as mentally ill (as you may know, for the media it is only brown or black-skinned people who are motivated by race or religious hatred, white people are always mentally ill). TICK, seen that.

iii) The EU Leave campaign will attack anyone who claims that the poisonous atmosphere of the referendum campaign may have contributed to the attack. TICK - some journalists have started to blog about this and have already been threatened.

It feels like a very dark day in Britain today. Yet the solution is not about a change here or a change there, it is about a wholesale commitment to remove violence from all that we do and intimidation from all that we say. That is the true pacifist cause.

21. Oswestry

"Toto, we're not in Wales anymore"

There was so much that was wrong at the time of my visit to Oswestry Meeting that I am not sure where to start. However, I hope that it will serve as a very good example of how a Quaker Meeting can be the perfect place to go at a time of change and uncertainty.

Let us start with why I was in north Wales[30]. I had worked for the Wales Council for Voluntary Action for seven years and part of my job had been travelling around Wales advising charities on how to integrate young volunteers into their workforce. I enjoyed the travel and seeing places that I would otherwise not have gone a great deal.

North and south Wales[31] may look close on a map, but the geography of Wales (plus its history) have made travel west and east far easier than travel north and south. For English readers, I would compare it to living in Southampton and visiting Newcastle or living in Carlisle and visiting Bristol. You can do these trips, but it is a major undertaking.

---

[30] I am hoping that this book will sell a few copies outside the UK, so perhaps for international readers I should note that at the time of writing the United Kingdom of Great Britain and Northern Ireland is made up on four parts - Wales, Scotland, England and Northern Ireland. Oswestry lies on the border of Wales and England, just on the English side.

[31] Please note that it is 'south Wales' or 'north Wales'. There is a habit in the English media of giving a capital letter to both words as if they are separate countries. They are not, 'south' and 'north' are simply descriptions of where in Wales you are talking about.

WCVA paid for me to travel around Wales, but it was always with work to do. Yes, I liked staying in Rhyl or Llandudno, but I never had the chance to be a tourist in either, let alone make a trip on the Welsh Highland Railway or any of the real tourist attractions of the area. When I left WCVA, I determined to take a holiday in north Wales and to see it as an outsider. A very good friend of mine agreed to come with me and we had the trip booked.

Several things happened in the meantime to change the circumstances of this trip. David Cameron (once Prime Minister of the UK for those reading later editions of this book when he has been forgotten) had decided to call a referendum on the UK's membership of the European Union (EU) on the day before my friend and I were due to set off on our travels in June 2016. It was no problem, we could vote and then meet that night to prepare to set off the next morning.

That Thursday night, my friend's mother fell seriously ill and he had to abandon the trip to head home. I was then faced with a week in hotels across north Wales with a spare bed and a much-amended itinerary. You can imagine that waking up on the Friday morning and starting the trip with the news that the UK had unexpectedly voted to leave the EU then also put a little bit of a shadow over the whole trip. It seemed that suddenly nothing was certain.

I do not want to let Brexit[32] dominate this chapter, but it is important. I remember sitting in Llanrhaeadr ym Mochnant watching the TV show 'The Last Leg' react with amazement to people who voted Leave searching 'What is the EU' online after the vote, I remember having

---

[32] The UK's decision to exit the EU. I look forward to the day when people have to look in the footnotes to find out what that words means.

breakfast in Llangollen reading about the huge surge in hate crimes after the vote as some people felt that they had the licence to abuse others again and I remember walking around Portmeirion reading about how a Welsh-speaking friend of mine had been threatened in the street because a man heard her speaking in Welsh to her child and assumed that she was Polish.

You can guess from this that I was not a Leave voter. That is important for this story, but I do want to emphasise that I have met Quakers who are passionate Leave supporters and see it as a natural part of their faith as much as I thought that my own faith would lead me to a Remain vote. There are different views on this but for this chapter to make sense, you have to imagine that I was particularly unhappy and lost (emotionally if not geographically) at this time.

Did I also mention that I had not long previously been dumped by a girlfriend and she was messaging me during my journey too?

After the initial visit to Llanrhaeadr ym Mochnant and then Pontcysyllte, I moved on to Llangollen. I had suggested a stop in Llangollen on the Sunday when I had been planning this trip with my absent friend, as we would be able to attend the Quaker Meeting there. Did we make it? Is this chapter called 'Llangollen'?

Checking the Meeting House door on the Saturday night, I realised that I had the wrong weekend and that it was a fourth Sunday rather than a third Sunday. There would be no Meeting in Llangollen the next day. Luckily, I knew that there was a Meeting in Oswestry ... over the border.

The border between Wales and England was not finally settled until the 19th century and then it was settled with English interests in mind. A friend of mine who is an expert in agriculture once told me that you could draw a line around all the most profitable land in the borders and know that that was where the English drew the line. It left some odd Welsh place names in England and you can still come across them if you drive around Shropshire. I challenge you to tell me that Bettws-y-Crwyn, Llanvair Waterdine, Llanymynech, Trefarclawdd and Argoed are ancient English names!

Oswestry, or Croesoswallt in Welsh, is one of those Welsh towns that ended up in England. Mind you, I have read that the name means 'Oswald's Cross' and refers to the King of Northumbria so perhaps we should acknowledge that things were a little less defined in previous eras. To this day though, you will find plenty of Welsh people and Welsh-speakers in Oswestry and even a few nostalgic ideas about bringing it back into Wales.

The funny thing is that the current structure of Quakers in Wales pays attention to this unusual set-up. It has not always been like this, but there are a number of Meetings in England which are nonetheless counted as part of Wales by Quakers and Oswestry is one of them. Despite being in Shropshire, Quakers in Oswestry are part of the 'North Wales Area' and would go to Area Meetings as far away as Bangor.

With no chance to go to Llangollen, I decided to take the trip to Oswestry and join them in trying to make sense of all the happenings of the past few days, both personal and political.

On arrival in Oswestry Meeting, I found that there had been a meeting of Friends in Wales the day before. Now I am overwhelming the non-Quaker readers with too much structure. For a proudly non-hierarchical tradition, Quakers sometimes seem to have a lot of structures! I will simplify things to the following -

Local Meeting - this is the local place where worship is held. All the places mentioned in this book are local Meetings. These are the basic building blocks of the structure.

Area Meeting - all the local Meetings are arranged into Areas. These are groups of Meetings that meet once a month to discuss business and oversee the Local Meetings. There are some things organised at an area level but beyond Oswestry being in North Wales Area[33], I am not sure I want to go any further down this route.

Friends in Wales - there is also an organisation which is based at a Wales level that meets three or four times a year to look at issues that are significant across Wales.

If I go into the structure of Quakers at a UK level then we could be here all night, so let me leave it at that. There had been a meeting of Friends in Wales on the Saturday after the Brexit referendum and it had been a place of shock, surprise and bewilderment.

I joined the Meeting and it was as interesting as any of those that I had been to and, once again, I was welcomed as a Friend and a visitor. At the end of the Meeting, there was a discussion about the events of the previous few days (political not personal events, though had people wanted to know my thoughts on nights out on your own in Llangollen, then that would have caused enough discussion).

I sat next to a Dutch man who worked at quite a high level in a local industrial firm. He and his family had lived in the UK for most of his adult life but now he regretfully informed the Meeting that he would have to leave. He loved the UK, but he wanted to live in Europe and the UK

---

[33] 'North Wales Area' is a title so you can use a capital letter for 'North' ... pedants please note!

had decided to leave Europe so he could not stay. It was sad and those who had known him in the Meeting for some time consoled him. He was not angry or bitter just disappointed and I thought of how those who became angry when they were served by a Polish waitress missed the point of how much of our economy was run by the work of people like this, people who would now leave the UK.

I should re-state that although everyone in this room was a supporter of the EU, I have since met Quakers who are not. I would say that the ratio is about 9 in every 10 Quakers being Remain voters, but there are some Leavers among the Society. I later met someone from the Oswestry Meeting who was a Leave voter and who had not been there on that day. I did not agree with him but I also hoped that he found a place in the Meeting, even if he was at odds with many of its members politically.

When it came to my turn to speak, I simply said something along these lines -

"We are Quakers. We are used to being in the minority. We were told that we were wrong to oppose slavery, but in the end others came round to our point of view. We were told that we were wrong to support equality of the sexes, but in the end others came round to our point of view. We were told that we were wrong to see equality of sexuality and to marry same sex couples, but now that is legal too. We are used to being in a minority and being told that we are wrong. Why are we now so worried that once again Quakers are in a minority and being told that we are wrong?"

I left Oswestry and returned to Llangollen, from where I was to head towards Lake Bala. I would love to tell you that the rest of the holiday passed without any further political incident, but there was more to come. However, in confusing and strange times, it was wonderful to be welcomed into the Oswestry community. I even spoke a little bit of Welsh with some people there. Well, it is only polite when you are in England.

It was a very confusing week.

22. Friends House Euston London

"The Mothership"

What does a Quaker Meeting House look like? You might think that no two look the same. That would be odd – churches are recognisably churches (or 'steeplehouses' as some of the early Quakers called them). Most of the time when you see a church, you know that it is a church. You might think that all Meeting Houses look like the one in your town or in the nearest city. That would be odd too - churches come in a range of styles that tell you when the church was built, often by whom and why. Travelling in northern Spain, I stopped in the cathedral town of Leon and was amused when the cathedral guide said 'you might be surprised to find a Gothic cathedral in Spain'. Up until that point, I had not considered architectural styles of Spanish churches at all.

There is always a delight in going to a new Meeting House (new to me, that is) and wondering what it will look like. Location is often the first thing. I expect older Meeting Houses to be in town and city centres and those that look like community centres to be out in a suburb dating to the 1950s or 1960s. If they are in a large suburb, then they are more likely to be a house left in someone's will for conversion into a Meeting House.

You can become obsessed with Meeting Houses themselves and that is obviously a distraction from the message of the worship. When I lived in Durham, local churchgoers sometimes derided those who worshipped at the city's huge cathedral as 'people who worship the cathedral rather than God'. Though I always found that unfair (hey, some of us need a cathedral to inspire us!), it did make a valid point and I have been interested to hear how many people have assumed that part of my Travelling Quaker project has been to compare the Meeting Houses themselves.

After seeing a few, I started to put them into categories. Firstly, there are those that are conference centres – walk into York or Birmingham Bull Street and you know that you are in a building that caters for business meetings. I have no objection to this and it find it a wonderful nod back to the Quaker tradition of competence in business. There are those like Bridgend and Portsmouth that are in former houses for the reasons noted above. However, most are hard to fit into a category, rather like Quakers themselves.

This brings me to the question of what you would expect Friends House in Euston, London to look like. We know that it will be old because property on Euston Road has presumably not come up for sale in recent times. I have heard at conferences of the Quaker bookshop or the Quaker café there so I imagined that it would have to be a big building, but what would you expect it to look like?

I will admit that I first went to Friends House several years ago, so I knew what it was going to look like. However, I know that others are surprised to find a rather grand Victorian structure with rather magnificent Roman columns along the front. Inside, there has been a considerable makeover so that it looks like a conference centre and the Sunday worship takes place in a room that would not have been out of place in any community centre. There is an odd contradiction in this – on the one hand, the grand outside can strike you as odd for the Quakers who value simplicity and yet on the other hand the lack of grandeur inside can leave you asking how this could be the HQ for Quakerism in the UK.

It seems like an obvious contradiction. If Quakers are directly inspired by the Spirit and this is channelled through their Local Meeting, then why is there any need for a central Quaker organisation? We understand that Roman Catholicism needs an HQ in Vatican City because the Pope is infallible when he sits on St Peter's Throne. We know that the Archbishop of Canterbury seeks to speak for the world's Anglicans. However, if your revelation on a wet Sunday morning in Eastbourne is as relevant as George Fox's (or anyone's), then why do we need a central HQ?

I had been to Friends House several times for conferences before I attended a Meeting there. To be honest, I did not question it at first. However, walking to Meeting in Euston on a Sunday morning, it occurred to me how atypical Friends House is. There is something about that grandness on the outside which should perhaps strike us as a little surprising. Then again, the obvious question about it is – how would you build a Quaker HQ in Euston?

I think that it is also a mistake to think of Friends House as an HQ in the same sense as other religious groups have HQs. In fact, I think that it is a mistake that Quakers themselves make from time to time. When we were organising a protest against an Arms Fayre in Cardiff, I suggested that I wrote a press release to notify the local newspapers of what we were going to do. I was told that I needed to contact Friends House before putting out any statement on behalf of Quakers. This would sound logical to anyone who has worked in a hierarchical structure or management – if you are way down the corporate ladder, you always need the approval of someone senior to you before you do anything.

The reaction from Friends House when I contacted the press officer there was – let us have a copy of the press release when it is done and we can help you circulate it. There was no permission needed, as long as the Elders of the Meeting had agreed the statement, then that was all the approval that was needed. I had suspected it might be like that because I had observed Friends House employees at conferences and noted that they are never there to direct proceedings and that they spend just as much time listening as talking.

This is not to say that Quakers do not have the same tendency towards hierarchy that other religions have. I have been at an Area Meeting where a 'weighty Friend' (not a phrase I like, all Friends are weighty) took me to task for my views on the role of Elders. To me, our equality as Quakers should have been more evident to her. I have also been told that recently Friends House renamed its secretarial roles to titles such as 'Head of Worship'. One has to ask whether Quakers should have a Head of Worship or perhaps a Heart of Worship?

How then do I describe my visit to The Mothership of Quakerism? Being met at the door and directed to the George Fox Room was a good start. Then I was surprised at how few Quakers were there for Meeting. It was an odd thing really, I had expected that HQ would be full of hundreds of Quakers. Perhaps that was unreasonable given how many Meetings there are in London. I also realised at the end of the Meeting that around half of those there were visitors from around the world.

As I wrote in the chapter on Streatham & Brixton, there is a certain connectedness about being a Quaker that I have never found in any other religious group where you can walk into a Meeting and be greeted as 'friend'. This then extends around the world and I suppose that it is our most basic statement of equality. I spoke to a young woman who had just moved to the UK from southern California and had made her first stop on a Sunday, a Meeting at Friends House. I asked her what she was looking forward to in the UK and she asked if it would rain during her four month stay. It was lovely to meet someone who was not going to be disappointed with the UK.

It might seem like a contradiction, but in many ways Quakers do manage the tensions between a central HQ and the rest of an organisation well. I mentioned in the introduction that my mother asked me who did the teaching in a Quaker Meeting. Although my answer at the time was that everyone does, I might have quoted a Quaker who was asked who chaired Quaker Business Meetings and who replied, 'Jesus Christ'. I once told this to my brother (a Roman Catholic) and he said that all Christian groups would say this. However, if I had to say whether my brother would be taken as more of an authority on Christian matters or the Pope, I can guess what I would say.

We are straying into the area of equality here and that is dealt with in another chapter. However, Friends House is a wonderful building and I encourage you to go there, both to see its grand exterior and its rather more restrained interior. I am told that this interior stands in stark contrast to the interiors of surrounding buildings and also that a major makeover was needed around 1990 to remove things like wooden benches covered in white rhino hide. I have also been told that the Meeting at Friends House has long stood as a welcoming place for LGBT Quakers and has a particular reputation for that aspect of equality. I am sure that the influence of so many visitors and so many people from around the world must help create that atmosphere.

However, there is a sense in which every Quaker Meeting is its own central HQ or should aspire to be so. There is no typical Quaker Meeting House, there is no typical Quaker. At least, if there ever is, then we are no longer Quakers.

23 Cardiff

"Home"

I am not sure if Quakers have a 'home' Meeting. In some areas it will be an odder concept than others. I had no choice in Cardiff because there was only one Meeting in the city, but on a visit to Birmingham I was once shown three Meeting Houses within a short walking distance of the Cadbury factory.

However, when I left Cardiff and found myself living closer to Bridgend Meeting than Cardiff Meeting, I did feel that I had a choice to make and I chose to carry on going to Cardiff. There is a sense of community to a Quaker Meeting which means that changing Meeting is as major disruption as moving house to a new area where you need to make new friends ... new Friends.

It seems only fitting then that I finish this story of my travels with the story of how I came to be part of Cardiff Meeting. I am touched and surprised when people ask me if I am a 'birthright Quaker' (born into a Quaker family and brought up in a Meeting) or suggest that I must have twenty or thirty years of Quaker experience behind me because no, I am a recent attender.

I put my interest in Quakerism (and we could do a whole different chapter on whether it is an 'ism') down to reading three books in around 2010 and a trip to a friend's wedding in Malta. As conversion experiences go, this is pretty off-beat! My entry point to Quakers came through the peace testimony, though I had always had a spiritual side and you might say that I had been looking for a way to engage in religion for some time.

The first book was Chris Mullin's diaries from his time as an MP in the Blair governments of 1997 to 2007. These are worth reading for their political intrigue, but I was very struck by his writings about his work as Chair of the Defence Select Committee. Just prior to the invasion of Iraq, they had asked the Head of MI6 if an invasion of Iraq would make the UK more or less dangerous for the average citizen. She replied – without hesitation – 'more dangerous'.

It really struck me that there was something odd about a government whose own security services were telling them that the course of action that they were pursuing would endanger their citizens and yet they pursued it with zeal.

This also chimed with something that I had read about in Tony Benn's diaries. I recommend Tony Benn's diaries for anyone who enjoys political memoirs. You do not have to agree with his conclusions, but his interest in politics and his belief in decent and reasoned political debate based on thinking through issues are a much needed antidote to current politics. Benn was, of course, involved in the Stop the War coalition and he makes the point that when this started it was impossible to get publicity for it but that slowly it grew to a point where broadcasters always wanted their opinion and everyone was claiming to have always been behind their campaign. It was progress from being ignored to being ridiculed to be accepted.

Again, I thought about unpopular causes. Our society is built on the works of people who took unpopular ideas – abolishing slavery, votes for women, freedom of speech for instance – and made them popular. What had I done?

Had I waited for causes to become popular before joining them? I examined my own conscience.

The third book was Naomi Klein's "The Shock Doctrine". This is a clearly political book and you may have to take some of it with a pinch of the author's prejudice but, my goodness, everyone should read the chapter on Iraq. You can follow her references and find out just how much money was made by American companies building US bases in Iraq or how the US strategy involved destroying the mobile phone network in Iraq even though they knew that Saddam Hussein and his regime did not use it. Start to do some research into how US troops were ordered to stop local communities organising votes and democratic elections, along with the elections that were cancelled when people voted to take control of the country's oil wealth out of the hands of American companies and you start to realise the degree to which a country and its society were destroyed for questionable aims.

However, all these three books did not just make me angry, they made me question who I was and what I was doing. I had heard bishops and Archbishops support the invasion of Iraq, where were the people who would say that killing other human-beings was not part of God's work? In Malta, I looked at the tombs in Valletta cathedral which showed angels stamping on turbans and I realised that religion had always been tied up in violence in this way.

Rather than despairing of religion though, I started searching for peace groups and campaigners. This was how I came across Quakers, a group who I probably thought had died out some centuries ago. I wrote to Friends House (if you are reading the chapters in the wrong order, this is Quaker HQ in London) and asked for information. They duly sent me books to read and I started to think about making a visit to my nearest Meeting – in Cardiff.

It took me a while to get there. I went and looked at the Meeting House a few times on a Saturday so that I knew where it was and I had to ring the Clerk to ask what was required of me. If Janet Felce had not been so generous with her time on the phone that day I might not have turned up to my first Meeting. I rarely name people in this book, but I feel that Janet deserves a special mention.

What happened when I first went along to a Meeting? It was odd. I had a whistlestop tour of the building and then I was invited to go into the Meeting Room and sit. This I did and enjoyed the silence and the peace of the Meeting. I am not sure that I grasped what was going on immediately, but I had time to pray and think about what I was doing.

After my first Meeting, I do remember talking to a man about his experiences in Edinburgh. Indeed, I was to find that this sociable part after Meeting was one of the things that I enjoyed about the experience in a way that I had not found in Churches. I enjoyed being there and I enjoyed the chance to chat to God about all sorts of things, including my writing ('get on with it' was the message).

I would love to tell you that after that I was a regular visitor and that everything has been happy and lovely since. It has most definitely not been happy and lovely either inside or outside the Meeting.

There were a couple of times when I had a month or two without going to Meeting. Usually this was accidental or a combination of events, but both times I returned for someone to ask me if I had been okay and to make a friendly enquiry about my absence. No-one should under-rate how important those approaches are to maintaining someone's interest in a Quaker Meeting.

I have only ever come close to not going back at all on one occasion. It was during the early days of the Meeting House refurbishment. You can read more about this in the next chapter, but for now let us say that there were firm views on all sides as to how we should go about the refurbishment. The disagreement was held very much in a Quaker way, but I did feel as though the Meeting was heading in a direction that I could not support.

The more that I considered this, the more that I felt that I could not stay within the Meeting. It was not the particular personalities involved (though also never under-rate the capacity of peaceful, 'that of God in everyone' Quakers to fall out with each other), I simply felt that the Meeting had moved in a direction which I did not feel was what we were being guided to do. In those circumstances, I felt that I ought to leave and worship elsewhere.

Before taking such a dramatic step, I prayed of course. I felt out of sorts but I also did not want to lose that connection to being a Quaker and the Quaker way of worship. It was then that I received an invite asking me to be an Elder of the Meeting. I supposed that I had my answer and it was for me to be more involved. I do think that the Meeting House refurbishment (for which this book raises money, see the next chapter and give generously) has developed in a very interesting way and so perhaps there was a resolution of all those strong opinions.

I suppose that we do all have a 'home' Meeting and mine is Cardiff. However, as I wrote in the chapter about Streatham & Brixton Meeting, one of the joys of any Quaker Meeting is that everyone who enters is among Friends.

I cannot tell you how many times I have been to Cardiff Meeting, but each occasion has been different. If you are ever in the city on a Sunday morning, come and meet us!

EPILOGUE

Before we go to the details of the Meeting House appeal and what is going to happen to the profits from this book, I feel as though I ought to add in an afterword about some of my travels.

The first thing to write is that there is no over-riding reason why I left out Reading, Fareham, South Belfast, Bridgend, Bath, Lancaster, Liverpool or Portsmouth. You will have read references to all of them in passing, but they all deserve their own chapters.

At some point in the future I will write about finding Reading Meeting House and how someone there recognised me from Cardiff Meeting about a year previously. Indeed, the photo on the front cover of the book was taken in Reading.

Then there is Fareham, a small Meeting tucked away in the back of a church which I found on a very wet Friday night two days before Christmas. They were an outreach project of Portsmouth Meeting and had once met in a café, an activity that could be challenging for both the public and Quakers.

Ah yes, Portsmouth Meeting, where I learned that they were part of the same 'Area Meeting' as the Channel Islands on the other side of the Channel but not Chichester Meeting just down the road. I also heard the wonderful story of a man who wrote to the Royal Navy after the Second World War to tell them that he was a pacifist and would not fight in any wars, only to be told that the Royal Navy does not recognise that pacifists exist.

You have read earlier about meeting a Quaker Buddhist in South Belfast Meeting (or perhaps Buddhist Quaker) but I will tell you at some point about how one of my friends dragged along to that Meeting with me took a new direction in her life after the experience. I also learned the importance of whether you use the 'purple book' or the 'red book' in Ireland. If you do not know what I mean by that, go back and read the chapter on Birmingham Bull Street.

Lancaster also crops up in the story about being prepared and the breaking of the bread in the Meeting House. It was also where I travelled from when I went to Yealand Conyers and was not mugged on the way there or back. That was another one where I would like to return some day or perhaps I will go when I finally do my 1652 Pilgrimage (not that I believe in pilgrimage, of course).

Liverpool taught me a lot about stoicism of a kind that we all need in Cardiff - was it three times that the Meeting House had been compulsorily purchased by the local authority as part of city centre redevelopment? Certainly they had had to change and adapt to circumstances outside their control.

Bath and Bridgend have their charms to write about as well. Bridgend amazed me with the commitment of its members to international development and Bath was in a grand Georgian building but still felt very down-to-earth and had a wonderful children's Meeting.

In other words, I am starting on another set of chapters for the second volume and no-one from those Meetings should feel slighted by the fact that they did not make it into this volume.

The second thing is that there are no grand conclusions from all this. We do tend to like grand conclusions and a meaning once we reach the end of the book. At school I was warned against viewing poems as Christmas crackers which you just had to pull the right way for the meaning to fall out (or a party hat falls out along with the meaning, unless the meaning is the party hat itself). This book is rather similar. I emphasise that everything is changing and that we are on a constant journey. I may well disagree with much of what I have written in a few years' time. The crucial thing for me is to stay open to change and not to join the inflexibility of so much of current debate.

However, I am going to observe that Quakers are both very similar and very different. There are no two Meeting Houses that felt similar and when I take my notes on each visit, I always note the Ministry, the welcome, the structure of the Meeting and no end of details that are different every time.

Yet, Quakers are also very similar to one another. There is always a welcome, an interest in visitors and an enthusiasm to talk about spiritual matters. Meetings for Business can be held in the middle of worship (as happened in Brixton) or after lunch (as happens in Cardiff) but they still run to the same formula (and the Treasurer always looks worried). Even when we disagree about things, there is something that we have in common as Quakers that also binds us together. I have never met anyone in a Quaker Meeting and thought 'you can't be a Quaker'.

Many years ago when I studied politics (do not ask me to explain current politics please), I learned about 'natural law'. This was a concept whereby human beings organised themselves by agreed rules but without anyone knowing that they were agreeing rules.

An example was that if you go to the hairdressers', you know that you have to wait your turn. You know when to queue for a bus and you know when it is your turn to be served at the bar. You might think that all this is politeness, but it is an unspoken way that we organise ourselves and it just works (go and push in a queue at the supermarket and see if people accept it as just another way of organising things).

I tend to think that there is a Natural Law at work within Quaker Meetings. Yes, we have Quaker Faith & Practice and yes we have the experience of our Elders, but I think that somehow we also evolve how we talk to one another and organise ourselves in such a way that anyone going to any Quaker Meeting can recognise something of how things 'should be'.

When I worked in youth work, we used to talk about 'the golden thread' in every young person. In other words, however much society had devalued and demoralised each young person, there was always something within them that we could connect with and possibly use to help them develop their talents to their full potential.

I am not saying that Quakers have a golden thread, more that travelling around makes you realise the degree to which we are organised by that of God in everyone.

24. Cardiff Meeting Appeal

Well done, you have read to this point unless, of course, you have just opened the book at the end to find out whodunnit. I will tell you now, it was George Fox in the Meeting House with the Bible.

If you have read this far, then I hope that you have enjoyed it. I will continue to travel around the UK's Quaker Meeting Houses and continue to write about them, as well as write my own 'One Quaker &' series. The next edition will probably be longer!

I do want to make a serious point before we end, however. This book was conceived as a way of raising money for the Cardiff Quaker Meeting House Appeal. It was turned down by Quaker publishers and so I have had to publish it myself. This makes the cost of publishing high and the proceeds of publishing low. Hence, when I say that I will put all the proceeds from this book to the Quaker Meeting House Appeal, I am talking about 75p from a printed copy and £1.50 from a Kindle copy. Let us be honest, this is not much.

Therefore I would like to tell you a little bit about the Meeting House Appeal and why I think that you should go to its JustGiving site and make a donation of £4 for a printed copy bought online or £3 for a Kindle copy (and if you do, please make mention that the last chapter of this book told you to do it).

There have also been further developments while this book has been being written. If you want a completely up to date picture of where things stand with our appeal, then contact Cardiff Quakers directly using the details here -

https://www.quaker.org.uk/meetings/cardiff-caerdydd

Cardiff Quaker Meeting House, as you probably read in the chapter about it, is a Victorian structure close to the city centre that was originally built as a house. I have heard that at one time it was a rectory for a neighbouring church as well, but certainly the area around it has changed somewhat since it was built.

Cardiff is a mishmash of architectural styles and the Meeting House is on a Victorian backroad of small offices, restaurants and clubs. Someone has built 'the skyscraper' at the end of the road, a large box of student accommodation that we worry will block out light to our garden and a café has opened on the other side named 'Bombers' (there is some discussion about whether we should inform them of the peace testimony). However, its location has many advantages and the consensus over the years has been that we want to stay there.

There is another serious point to this. Cardiff Meeting House is host to a large number of voluntary sector organisations and meetings and, as such, is an important community hub. It is spread over four floors and groups include the Unitarian Church, local mental health services, the Amber Project for young self-harmers and Bi-Polar UK. I once opened the front door on the way to a Meeting to find a well-known celebrity standing on the other side of the door having just been to a depression support meeting. I am not going to tell you who that was of course, but I did consider that they felt that they could trust the Meeting House as a place to go for support.

However, the flipside of having an old building is the need for repair. It is also quite a difficult space for disabled access and can appear a little unwelcoming as the entrance is through a narrow door at the side of the building. We make the best of it, but we would like to do so much more.

Originally, the Meeting looked at two plans. One would involve the building of a new Meeting room on the back of the building to accommodate a bigger Meeting and also to allow us to sit in a proper circle during Meeting (instead of a U shape). The other was a less ambitious plan to solve the access and welcome issues with the option left open to build a new Meeting room in future years. There was much discussion (or should I write discernment) over a number of years and the initial scheme was accepted with further thought to take place about the more ambitious work.

To give you an idea of our starting point, for some things it has been bringing the building into the twentieth century – believe it or not, the initial stages of the appeal funded double glazing and heating in some rooms!

All this comes at a price - £200,000 at the last count. We have a Fundraising Team working on big bids to government and major charities to support this, but we need all the help that we can get from those who support our aim of continuing and enhancing this community provision (as well as Quaker worship).

If I tell you how much has been raised to date then it will be out of date the moment that the book is printed but I can say that when I wrote this chapter, there was a long way to go towards £200,000.

So ...

Please go to our JustGiving site to donate ...

https://www.justgiving.com/crowdfunding/cardiffquakermeetinghouseappeal

Or why not set up a standing order to pay a small amount each month? You can contact us at through www.quakers.org.uk to find out more.

However ...

If you do look at the picture of the Meeting House on the quaker.org website then you can just see a small office building to the right of the picture. These are some offices dating from the 1990s which were built in the same style as the rest of the street. During 2018, there was publicity about them being sold as a site for a development of luxury flats.

At the time of writing, we are in discussion with the developers as to how we might work with them so as to maximise what we want to do with the site. However, this does not mean that anyone is going to hand us a blank cheque for building work that is needed so please do go and click on the justgiving link still.

Obviously in the second edition I will update you as to what is happening!

In the meantime, thank you for reading and I hope that I will see you in the second edition. There are still another 380 Meeting Houses to visit and 388 write-ups to do still.

In Friendship

Dewi

p.s. if you bought the book from me directly for a fiver then you have already given £5 ... by why stop there?

And if you want to complain, praise or generally take issue with anything I write, then feel free to contact me at dewiheald@gmail.com

Photos of Meeting Houses

The point of this book is not the Meeting Houses themselves, but here for the record are some photographs of some of those that I have visited.

Please note that if you have a Kindle or e-book version of this book then these may not show correctly and you may just see some blank pages!

Eastbourne Meeting House

Aberystwyth Meeting House

Swansea Meeting House

Friends House, London

Quaker Burial Ground in Quakers Yard, Rhondda Cynon Taff

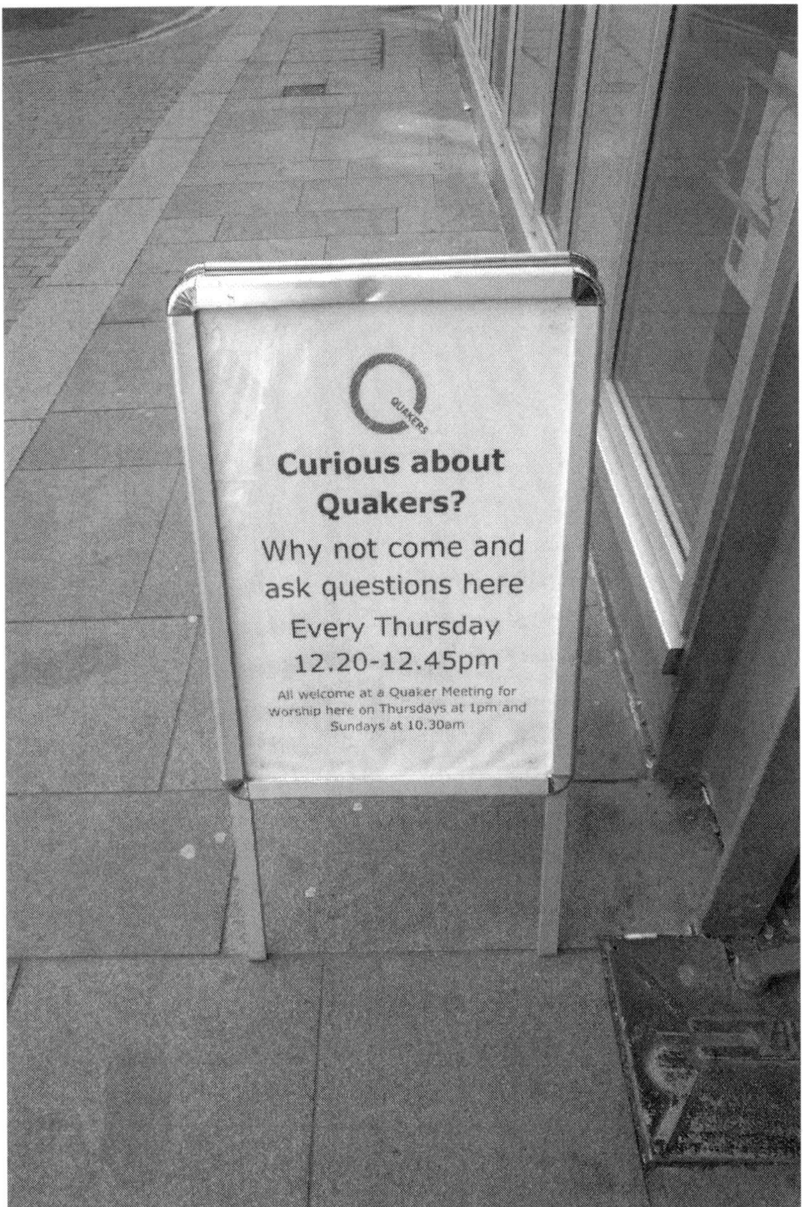
QUAKERS
Curious about Quakers?
Why not come and ask questions here
Every Thursday 12.20-12.45pm
All welcome at a Quaker Meeting for Worship here on Thursdays at 1pm and Sundays at 10.30am

23265989R00086

Printed in Great Britain
by Amazon